Praise for

Inclusion Body Myositis: A Guide for Patients

"Bill Tillier's book about the practical aspects of living with inclusion body myositis can be helpful for those with newly diagnosed disease as well as those with advanced disease. Recognizing that each patient experiences their inclusion body myositis journey at a different pace and may have varied concerns, this is a good resource divided by topic that explains the illness in depth and can serve as an instructive guide for patients who wonder how to navigate certain situations. Given that he himself has lived through the challenges of navigating his own illness, he provides an insightful insider's view to help others who may be experiencing similar challenges. I think this book can serve as an important extension of information beyond the clinic visit with a doctor."

~ **Lisa Christopher–Stine, MD, MPH**, Professor of Medicine Director, Johns Hopkins Myositis Center"

"Thanks to Bill Tillier, a long-time Science Advisor for MSU, we now have an easy-to-understand book all about Inclusion Body Myositis. This book will help patients with IBM and care partners better adapt to a life with IBM. Bill, a retired psychologist, opens up about his journey throughout the book, providing helpful tips on how to handle the needs of this rare disease over time. Bill's candid discussion of the psychological aspects of coping with IBM brings a dimension to the book rarely talked about. I consider this a 'must-read!'"

~ **Jerry Williams,** Founder and President, Myositis Support and Understanding

Inclusion Body Myositis

A Guide for Patients

Inclusion Body Myositis
A Guide for Patients

William Tillier, M.Sc.

Foreword by

Dr. S. A. Greenberg

Inclusion Body Myositis: A Guide for Patients

Contact the author: btillier@shaw.ca
Author website: http://www.ibmmyositis.com/

Editor: Chris Nelson

ISBN:
978-1-7781138-0-2 (ebook)
978-1-7781138-1-9 (Paperback)

Calgary, Alberta Canada

DISCLAIMER

This book details the author's personal experiences with, research on, and opinions about Inclusion Body Myositis (IBM) and related topics. The author is a person with IBM, not a health care provider. This book is not intended to diagnose, treat, cure, or prevent any condition or disease. Please consult with your own physician or health care specialist regarding the suggestions and recommendations made in this book.

Before you begin any health-related program or change your lifestyle in any way, you should consult your physician or other licensed health care practitioners.

Neither the author nor publisher nor other representatives will be liable for damages arising out of or in connection with the use of this book. This is a comprehensive limitation of liability that applies to all damages of any kind. The use of this book implies your acceptance of this disclaimer.

DEDICATION

I dedicate this book to my wife, Angela. Without her tremendous support and love, I certainly could not accomplish what I do.

TABLE OF CONTENTS

A NOTE ON FORMATTING

The material in text boxes is either presented as background information or represents a bit more complicated explanation.

Paragraphs presented in italics represent the personal experiences of the author.

FOREWORD

Approximately 50 years ago, the medical profession noticed that some patients with what was called polymyositis in fact had a different disease, which we now call inclusion body myositis (IBM). A large body of medical literature, with an estimated 2,000 publications in medical journals, about this disease has since been produced. Although the medical profession, and myself as part of it, have some understanding of how this disease affects the patients we treat, our perspective is limited.

For almost 2 decades, Bill Tillier has provided resources and support to the IBM community through his efforts, including his website www.ibmmyositis.com. Here, Bill has produced a monograph detailing the perspectives of patients with IBM. This remarkable volume covers views well known to the medical profession (e.g., patient demographics, clinical manifestations, theories of cause, and treatment issues), but also discusses the issues most important to people with IBM that are less discussed by and sometimes little known by, IBM medical professionals. The discussions on complications directly connected to IBM (Chapter 2), physical adaptation (Chapter 5), and psychological aspects (Chapter 6) are particularly practical and helpful.

I am very grateful to Bill for his efforts and hope that together we find treatments for IBM as soon as possible.

Steven A Greenberg, MD
sagreenberg@bwh.harvard.edu

CHAPTER 1: OVERVIEW OF IBM

This monograph overviews a strange and rare muscle disease called inclusion body myositis (IBM). It is written for the average patient with IBM to help them better understand the condition and suggest how best to cope with it. It is being written by a patient with IBM diagnosed in 2002. The book should be helpful to patients, their doctors and families, and to caregivers as well. I have used straightforward ideas and language.

I provide insight derived from my own experience and information about IBM obtained from various sources. While most patients generally benefit from knowledge about IBM, I want to emphasize that information is no substitute for an ongoing relationship with a physician and, ideally, a medical team. Every case is unique and must be carefully evaluated by competent physicians. I highly discourage anyone who attempts to treat themselves or who acts against competent medical advice.

Chapter 1 describes the main characteristics of the disease and who gets it. Chapter 2 examines complications commonly seen in the course of the illness. Chapter 3 highlights diagnosis and the lack of treatment available. The causes of IBM and research are discussed in Chapter 4. I consider the need for physical adaptation and management in Chapter 5. Chapter 6 reviews the psychological aspects of coping with IBM. Chapter 7 provides further resources to assist the patient with IBM.

1.1 A GENERAL OVERVIEW

Inclusion body myositis (IBM) is an extremely rare, serious, chronic, progressive disease. Rare means very few people develop the disease. It is considered a serious disease because it often leads to severe impairment of mobility and day-to-day function. Chronic means that once it starts, it does not go away. Progressive means that you slowly get worse and worse over time. At the time of this writing there are no therapies available for IBM.

A frustrating aspect of IBM is that it is variable and impacts people in different ways, at different ages, and at different rates. This makes it harder for doctors to diagnose.

IBM strikes and kills the cells of specific muscles, leading to those muscles becoming weaker and weaker. The disease is complex. Doctors do not know what causes it, and they have not been able to develop a treatment that will help.

There are five common complications seen in IBM: weakness in the throat, often causing problems swallowing and resulting in choking, weakening of the muscles involved in breathing, excess mucus buildup, and pain, which can be intense. Finally, many patients complain of chronic exhaustion.

The condition is very frustrating for patients because it slowly robs us of our abilities to do everyday things in life; for example, it often makes walking difficult or impossible. Weakness in the arms and hands makes it difficult to pick up items or use everyday objects.

Until doctors can discover a treatment, the focus of the patient must be on adapting to and managing everyday physical challenges and learning to cope with the illness psychologically. It can be frustrating and disheartening to lose function; keeping a realistic but positive attitude is critical. For a comprehensive, recent review of IBM, see the article by Naddaf (2022). This study is available to the public (see the reference section in chapter 7).

1.1.1 The name and classification

Diseases are usually named after the doctor who discovered them (e.g., Alzheimer's, Parkinson's) or based on the impact seen in the body (e.g., multiple sclerosis, where "sclerosis" means the tissue has become scarred, hard and fibrous). The name "inclusion body myositis" was first used in 1971, and research has been ongoing since then. It's called myositis because it involves an inflammation of the muscles: "*myo*" means muscle, and "*itis*" means inflammation, just as appendicitis implies inflammation of the appendix. It's called "inclusion body" because, under the microscope, the muscles often show small, abnormal lumps that the doctors call inclusion bodies. These lumps are formed from abnormal proteins. The muscle also sometimes shows characteristic holes called "rimmed vacuoles." Because the disease strikes "out of the blue," it is often referred to as sporadic. When reading about IBM, you will often see it called sporadic inclusion body myositis or sIBM.

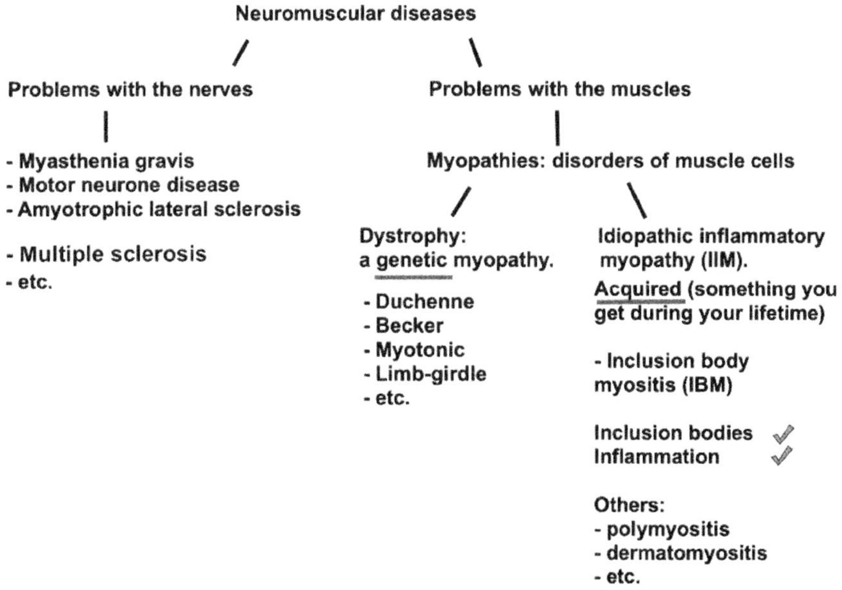

Figure 1 Classification.

IBM is classified as a type of idiopathic inflammatory myopathy (IIM). Idiopathic means that they don't know what causes it. Myopathy is a disease of the muscle cells that causes weakness. IBM is often listed under the broad umbrella of muscular dystrophy disorders.1.1.2 A disease of aging.

IBM strikes people of different ages. Generally, the disease is not seen before the age of 40 (there are a few cases with people in their thirties), and it is associated with aging. On average, the age at which most patients develop IBM is between about 55 and 65. It is more common to see IBM in people as they get older. This means that the rate of IBM in a population will go up as the population gets older.

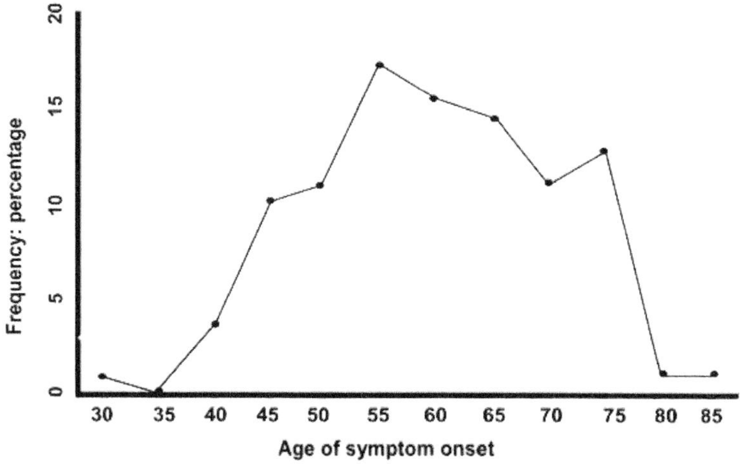

Figure 2 IBM and age of symptom onset. (After Greenberg, 2016).

In my case, when I first went to a neurologist at age 40 (in 1998), he said, "You couldn't have IBM because you are too young," but now it's recognized that some 20% of cases occur in people under the age of 50 (Greenberg, 2019).

1.1.3 Genetic predisposition.

IBM is not a genetic disease—it is not passed on to your children. Despite that, research has discovered that some people have a group of genes that may make them more likely to get IBM compared to people who do not have these genes. This is called a genetic predisposition.

IBM is most common in people whose ancestors originated in northern Europe. The genes that these people developed many generations ago seem to increase the likelihood of getting IBM today. Having these genes does not mean that you *will* develop IBM, but having these genes somehow makes it *more likely* to develop IBM than it is for people who do not have them. These genes also make it more likely to get other autoimmune-type disorders—for example, Crohn's disease or rheumatoid arthritis.

There is also an exceedingly rare form of IBM called familial IBM (fIBM) that may occur in relatives in your family in the same generation. These cases are *not* passed on to children.

1.1.4 Impact of IBM on lifespan.

The question concerning the impact of IBM on one's lifespan is a critical one for patients. Unfortunately, this is a complicated question to answer for several reasons. Statistics concerning the cause of death in IBM are challenging to interpret, in part because most studies only look at a small number of patients. Not enough research has been completed. IBM is an extraordinarily rare disease. "IBM age of onset is late, and many patients at the time of diagnosis have already exceeded average life-span" (Greenberg, 2021, p. 5). Finally, the cause of death numbers may be thrown off (made worse) by some patients with IBM who do not identify or manage complications well.

In the past, it was believed that IBM does not impact longevity (how long people live). Doctors have now studied a group of patients with

IBM in several counties in Minnesota and Wisconsin. These studies (Naddaf et al., 2021; Shelly et al., 2021) reveal preliminary but essential insights into the problems that patients with IBM may develop and the impact of IBM on longevity. Here is a summary of the recent study done by Naddaf et al. (2021).

- The study involved 50 patients with IBM.
- Survival was decreased in patients with IBM by an average of three years compared to the overall population.
- Weakness in swallowing was the most common complication (64% of patients with IBM).
- Respiratory failure or pneumonia was the most common cause of death (44%).

These results are similar to those reported by Shelly et al. (2021). That study found that patients with IBM' median age of death was 84 years, compared to a non-IBM population of 87.5. Shelly et al. (2021) studied 21 cases. Thirteen patients died; nine, or 69%, were related to IBM (three from aspiration pneumonia, four from respiratory failure, two unspecified). Shelly et al. (2021) found that when death could be blamed directly on IBM, it was predicted by three factors: the presence of swallowing weakness, being female, and having a diagnosis after the age of 67.

In the latest study, Brokamp et al. (2022) reviewed 54 patients with IBM. They found that 59% showed forced vital capacity deficits, a critical measure of lung function, and they recommended initial and ongoing pulmonary monitoring for patients with IBM. The study showed that patients who were initially assessed as being weaker experienced a faster pulmonary decline. Still, limb muscle weakness was not correlated with respiratory weakness (progression rates differ between limb and ventilatory muscle dysfunction). Finally, the study implied that those who do not initially have respiratory weakness may experience a slower disease progression.

The fact that respiratory failure and pneumonia were the most common causes of death emphasizes the importance of following up and carefully managing swallowing weakness and respiratory weakness, the two most common IBM complications.

Because IBM is a disease of aging, many people with IBM will die of age-related illnesses rather than directly from IBM. For example, today in the United States, the leading causes of death for persons over 65 are heart disease 32%, cancer 22%, stroke 8%, lower respiratory (CLRD) 6% influenza/pneumonia 3%, Alzheimer's 3%, diabetes 3%, kidney disease 2%, accidents 2%. That accounts for 81% of natural death causes (Gorina et al., 2006).

Nonetheless, we need to be aware of potential complications from IBM, and we need to watch ourselves for them. We need to be co-managers with our healthcare team in handling the issues that come up. It is wrong—the wrong perspective—to see IBM as a death sentence.

1.1.5 Just how rare is IBM?

Just what is a rare disease? A rare disease is defined differently, depending on where you live. In Canada, it is a disease affecting less than five people per hundred thousand. In the United States, it is a disease impacting less than 200,000 people.

With this said, for several reasons, it is challenging to say exactly how many people have developed IBM. We need more research to better understand this question; however, doing these studies is time-consuming and expensive. The disease is difficult to diagnose, and many older people who suffer from IBM never seek medical attention because they attribute the problems to "just getting old." Many more people likely have IBM than are diagnosed with it.

Because IBM is a disease associated with aging, if you survey only people in the population 30 years old or older, in 2010, the prevalence of IBM was 97.2 per million (Shelly et al., 2021). If you survey only people in the population 50 years old or older, the prevalence rises to about 182 people per million (Shelly et al., 2021). Greenberg (2021) estimates that there are 20,000 to 26,000 people with IBM in the USA today.

1.1.6 Comorbidities and IBM.

In this section, we are interested in what other diseases occur more often when you have IBM. This may help you connect the dots if you have some of these illnesses, but it is also an essential section for doctors monitoring patients with IBM.

Comorbidity is when a patient has a disease (IBM) and, on top of that, also has an additional disease (or diseases). The disorders may occur spontaneously and be independent of each other (e.g., IBM and prostate cancer) or may be causally related (e.g., IBM and rheumatoid arthritis). Comorbidities are not the same as complications: complications arise directly from the condition (we will look more closely at complications in Chapter 2). It is well-recognized that, in general, having comorbidities is related to aging, and it is not uncommon to see older adults having two or more chronic conditions.

Compared to a non-IBM population, IBM comorbidities include:

- Other autoimmune diseases were present in 48% of cases, often Sjogren's syndrome or rheumatoid arthritis (Shelly et al., 2021). Some 6% showed Sjögren's syndrome in the Naddaf et al. study (2021).
- Cardiovascular risk factors: hyperlipidemia (46.8% vs. 17.8%) and hypertension (65.9% vs. 22.3%) (Keshishian et al., 2018).
- Some 36% of patients with IBM showed peripheral

neuropathy (Naddaf et al., 2021).

- Diabetes mellitus (33.8% vs. 10.4) (Keshishian et al., 2018).
- Anemia (31.6% vs. 7.0%) (Keshishian et al., 2018).
- Muscle pain (myalgia and myositis, unspecified 28.3% vs. 0.8%) (Keshishian et al., 2018).
- Fatigue (19.1% vs. 3.4%) (Keshishian et al., 2018).
- Joint pain (arthralgia 15.2% vs. 4.1%) (Keshishian et al., 2018).
- Depression (14.4% vs. 3.2%) (Keshishian et al., 2018).
- Cardiovascular events: myocardial infarction (12.5% vs. 2.4%) and congestive heart failure (17.2% vs. 4.5%) (Keshishian et al., 2018).
- Pulmonary events (pneumonia 10.5% vs. 1.8% and aspiration pneumonia 5.8% vs. 0.3%) (Keshishian et al., 2018).
- Insomnia (5.3% vs. 0.6%) (Keshishian et al., 2018).

1.1.7 COVID–19 and IBM

COVID-19 stands for coronavirus disease 2019 (2019 is the year it was discovered). A virus named SARS-CoV-2 causes the disease; it stands for severe acute respiratory syndrome coronavirus 2. Most muscle-related associations advise those with neuromuscular disease to get vaccinated and have the associated boosters (e.g., The Myositis Association; Myositis Support and Understanding; Muscular Dystrophy Association USA; Muscular Dystrophy UK). This has also been supported by other organizations involved in muscle diseases. The rationale is that the risk of COVID-19 infections in those having muscle diseases outweighs the vaccine's potential risks (see Živković et al., 2021).

1.1.8 Miscellaneous information on IBM

Although patients often feel that the disease "goes up and down," research shows that it slowly progresses and is not known to go into remission.

For some unknown reason, IBM is twice as common in men. There will be an average of 67 men and 33 women for every hundred patients with IBM.

Research has confirmed that IBM does not impair thinking or memory functions.

As mentioned above, peripheral neuropathy was seen in 36% of IBM cases. Peripheral neuropathy involves weakness, numbness, and pain, usually in the hands and feet, caused by damage to the peripheral nerves.

Sjögren's syndrome was seen in 6% of patients with IBM. Sjögren's is an autoimmune, rheumatic disease characterized by dry eyes and mouth, fatigue, and pain. Sjögren's is much more common in women than men, and first onset is typically after age 40.

1.2 DIFFERENT MUSCLES, DIFFERENT PEOPLE.

Part of the complexity of IBM is that not all muscles are affected, and different groups of muscles are often affected at different times and at different rates. Heart muscle is not impacted. IBM does not "look the same" in all patients with IBM, and there is no one way that IBM starts or develops. There are many different ways that IBM can impact people, making it difficult to diagnose and making it difficult to compare yourself to other patients with IBM.

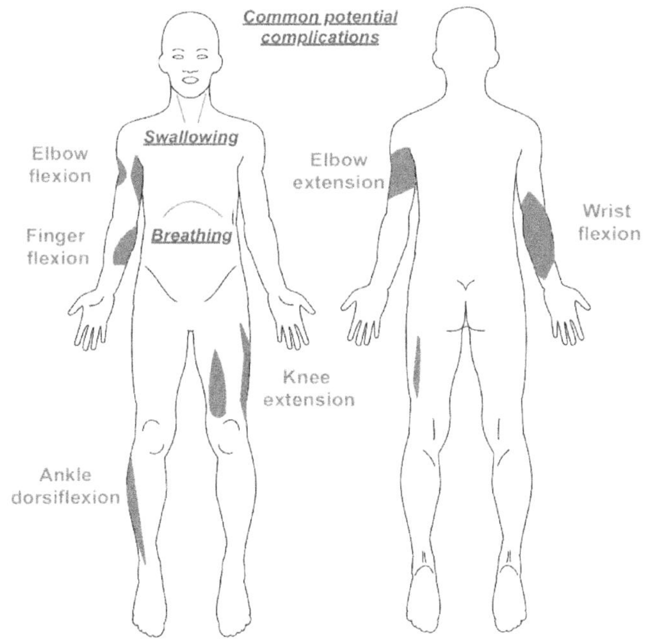

Figure 3 Common muscle groups impacted. (After Greenberg, 2019).

1.2.1 Specific muscles impacted

As shown in the diagram above, IBM tends to initially impact different groups of muscles. The way IBM develops varies widely—some individuals develop weakness in their arms and hands first, others in the legs first, and, for some, weakness in the arms and legs occurs together. In about 6 to 9% of patients with IBM, swallowing weakness is the first symptom to emerge, and some of these folks may not develop arm or leg muscle weakness for up to another 5 years (Shelly et al., 2021).

The weakness comes on very slowly, developing over a period of years. In many cases, IBM seems to impact one side of the body more than the other. If you are right-handed, it is typical for the left side of the body to be affected more severely (and vice versa).

1.2.2 Weakness in the arms

Weakness in the arms shows itself first in the hands. A typical first sign is noticing weakness in the thumb or forefinger (e.g., when pushing down on a spray can) or the little finger. Over time, it becomes challenging to make a fist, and you lose strength in the fingers (e.g., it can be hard to open a car door). You may progress to the point where you cannot pick up objects or write. Putting a box on a higher shelf becomes difficult. Weakness may progress to the point where it becomes impossible to lift your hand.

1.2.3 Weakness in the legs

Weakness in the legs is first focused on the large muscles in the front of the leg between the knee and the hip. These muscles are used in walking and in stabilizing the knee. They are also used, for example, to lift the lower leg and foot when sitting down in, or standing up from, a chair. They are the same muscles used in kicking a football or riding a bicycle.

> *In my case, I first noticed weakness in my legs when I did a deep knee bend to look at something inside a display counter at a store; I couldn't get up. Then I noticed that my finger was weak when I pushed down the button on my spray deodorant can. Later, I started to trip, and I fell many times.*

Climbing stairs becomes challenging as you find raising your leg high enough to get to the next step increasingly difficult, and eventually, it becomes impossible to use stairs. It also becomes more and more challenging to get up from ordinary chairs.

> *I got by for some time, taking one step at a time on stairs and using the handrail to pull myself up. I also had lots of trouble*

using ordinary chairs and resorted to using cushions to raise them higher. I was stuck several times, unable to get up, in restaurant chairs, and once on a church pew at a funeral.

1.2.4 Falling

Falls due to leg weakness are a widespread problem in IBM, especially in the early stages. Fall management involves becoming aware of the types of falls common in IBM and how best to prevent falls. Many patients experience frequent falling, often leading to substantial injuries.

Three types of falls are common. In the first type, the muscles supporting the knee fail, and the leg collapses. You quickly fall straight down — before having time to reach out to grab anything. These falls often result in injuries to the ankles.

The second type of fall occurs when you become unbalanced and fall over. The muscles cannot compensate quickly enough, and you slowly fall over, like a tree falling in the forest. These falls frequently occur on uneven ground (lawns, gravel) and often result in head injuries.

In the third type of fall, the muscles in the leg do not lift the toe high enough when stepping (called toe drop), which causes tripping. This is common when stepping up onto a curb, and the foot does not raise high enough, or, when walking in tall grass, the foot gets "caught," and you trip.

Being aware of falls, and preventing falls, is very important. Many patients use knee or ankle braces. Early in the disease, working with a physiotherapist on leg strengthening and fall prevention may be helpful.

I have had all three types of falls. Altogether, I probably fell thirty times (because I was slow to use a cane). In one case, I was walking between two vehicles in a parking lot and fell straight down so quickly that I didn't have time to grab the car's fender. Another time, I reached out to get the mail out of the box, lost my balance, and fell.

I was fortunate; I broke my ankle once and sustained a seventy-stitch cut on my arm. Many patients experience broken hips and concussions. I eventually used a cane and then a rollator. When I started to fall on top of my rollator, I realized that I needed a power wheelchair.

I would emphasize that walking aids are essential to use early on to *prevent* falling. Over time, using a cane, walker (rollator), or wheelchair may be required, depending upon how far the disease progresses.

1.3 INTRODUCTION: KEY POINTS

- IBM is an extraordinarily rare muscle disease.
- IBM usually weakens the arms and legs.
- Once you have IBM, it doesn't go away, and it slowly worsens.
- IBM has no known cause or treatment.
- Falling is a major early problem.
- About 20% of cases occur in patients in their forties.
- The majority of cases occur between the ages of 50 and 65.
- IBM likely has a genetic predisposition but is not passed on to children.
- IBM has been shown to shorten lifespan, on average, by three years.
- IBM commonly has complications: it may impact muscles involved in swallowing and breathing. Pain and excess

mucus may be present.

- Other autoimmune diseases occur in about 50% of patients with IBM.
- Coping with IBM is a psychological challenge.

CHAPTER 2: COMPLICATIONS

2.1 COMPLICATIONS DIRECTLY CONNECTED TO IBM

There are five significant complications directly related to IBM: weakness in the muscles used in swallowing and in breathing, excess mucus buildup, pain, and fatigue.

Because problems with swallowing and breathing significantly impact one's health, these are the most critical issues to watch for. Ideally, when you are first diagnosed, your breathing and swallowing should be evaluated to establish a baseline for you. You may have to ask for these examinations.

Learning about the complications of IBM is very important because your voice is the channel to let the doctor know how the disease progresses. Your doctor will rely upon you to keep them informed about what you are experiencing. Understanding and anticipating possible complications will allow for earlier detection of them if and when they arise. This, in turn, will support you and your doctor in the prompt assessment of problems and the creation of a management strategy for further care. Initially, this management strategy may be simply to keep an eye on the issue. Action may be taken depending on how serious it is, to begin with, and then depending on how it progresses.

Do you smoke? Do you drink? Are you overweight? If you develop IBM complications, these issues may impact you by making complications worse and more challenging to deal with.

Much can be done to manage these complications. It is also clear that if you do nothing and do not bring these problems to your doctor's attention, you will be jeopardizing yourself. IBM is the sort of disease where you have to do what you can *when* you can and try to accept those things that you can't do anything about.

2.1.1 Swallowing

Because of how the throat is built, you cannot breathe and swallow simultaneously; it is one or the other. Most of the time, we take swallowing for granted. In reality, a coordinated series of muscles is involved in moving the tongue and constricting the throat so that when we swallow food, it goes down "the right pipe." This involves three stages. The first stage consists of the tongue helping move food to the back of the throat. In the second stage, the little flap at the back of the throat (the epiglottis) moves, together with the voice box (larynx), to close and block food from going into the "air pipe" and the lungs. In the third stage, the food pipe (esophagus) squeezes (it has muscles) and pushes the food down towards the stomach.

Swallowing weakness is called dysphagia. Given the increased risks of aspiration pneumonia and death associated with swallowing weakness, I was surprised to read a 2019 article stating that this complication in IBM has only recently received much research attention (Mohannak et al.). This report emphasized the high number of patients with IBM who show swallowing weakness and highlighted that the early indications are ignored or not recognized in many cases. Mohannak et al. (2019) outlined four early indicators:

- The need to swallow repeatedly to get food down
- The need to wash food down with liquids
- Regurgitation of food
- Outright choking

They recommend that doctors be sensitized to routinely ask two questions: "Does food get stuck in your throat?" and "Do you have to swallow repeatedly to get rid of food?"

Studies show that from 10 to 50% of patients with IBM have swallowing issues when first diagnosed. About 40 to 80% of patients with IBM will develop significant weakness in the throat muscles during their disease, making this a frequent complication (Goyal & Mozaffar, 2021; Mohannak et al., 2019). The number of people with IBM who have swallowing weakness has been hard to estimate, and the current numbers are probably underestimated (Mohannak et al., 2019; Shelly et al., 2021). Swallowing weakness was the most common complication, seen in 64% of patients with IBM in the Naddaf et al. (2021) study and in 67% of cases in the Shelly et al. (2021) study.

Commonly, swallowing is first assessed by having a specialist, often a speech pathologist, watch you swallow. At the next level, swallowing is measured by drinking a barium solution while the doctor watches on an x-ray machine. If you have swallowing problems, your doctor may suggest various treatments.

Weakness in the swallowing muscles can cause coughing. If a small piece of food (even a grain of rice) gets caught in the wrong place in the throat, it triggers the coughing reflex, forcing you to cough to try to dislodge whatever is there. If you are coughing, the air goes back and forth, and you will make a noise that other people can hear.

Food may get caught in the throat, causing choking. Choking is a reflex that constricts and squeezes the throat shut. Choking can be partial, where some air is getting through (you try to cough), or total, where no air is getting through. In choking, the airflow is usually so reduced that the person can no longer speak or breathe (or make any sound at all).

You cannot control choking because it is a reflex: you cannot "force yourself" to stop choking. This is a medical emergency because we can only survive without air for a few minutes. It's not unusual for a person to panic when choking.

> *I have found that when I choke, panic makes it worse. When I feel I have problems and am about to choke, I try very hard to*

breathe slowly and stay calm. Sometimes you have no warning, and these have been my worst episodes.

Generally speaking, you need help to remove the stuck food. Those around you should lean you forward and give you up to five back blows between the shoulder blades if you are choking. This can be followed by up to five chest thrusts: the so-called Heimlich maneuver. The Heimlich maneuver forces air from your stomach up, pushing the blockage out. Usually, this maneuver is done by someone standing behind you and placing their arms around you. Pulling up on the stomach brings air up to push the blockage out. The Heimlich maneuver can also be done with someone sitting in a wheelchair by having someone stand behind and reach around and pull up on the person's abdomen. Another method is to have someone stand in front of the wheelchair and push on the abdomen of the person in the wheelchair to help bring material up.

If possible, try not to eat alone and sensitize your eating partners to your issues in advance. Tell them how you will signal them ahead of time. As mentioned above, when you choke, you cannot ask for help, and it may not be evident to them that you are choking: you usually can't make any noise at all. I suggest that if you choke, you should vigorously shake your shoulders to alert your eating partner that you have an issue; this should signal them to ask, "Are you choking?"

Sometimes you swallow, and the food does not go down entirely. You may not notice this and eat again. This may cause a lump of food to build up and "get stuck halfway down." This food either has to come back up or go down. If you're not careful, this blockage may cause you to choke.

In another situation, you choke, and food gets sucked into the air tube as you struggle to breathe, going into the lungs. This is called aspiration. Generally speaking, when this happens, the food in the lungs will cause pneumonia. This needs to be treated carefully, and it presents a risk of overwhelming the patient, leading to death.

Some patients have so many issues with choking that they eventually require a tube inserted into the abdomen to get nutrition (a "PEG tube"). In the Shelly et al. (2021) study, two-thirds of patients with IBM developed swallowing weakness, and half of them required a feeding tube, generally ten years after onset. Although this sounds frightening, many people have this and manage it well. After having a tube inserted, you may still be able to drink and swallow by mouth, especially if you focus on foods that are easier for you. This way, you can still enjoy participating in meals with friends and family.

You need to talk to your family and your doctor and get their help and advice in dealing with swallowing issues. Some patients have problems and become afraid to eat. Sadly, some patients with IBM do not seek help and die of malnutrition.

I am fortunate that I have not had significant problems swallowing. Even so, I notice that IBM has affected my swallowing and speaking ability (Sometimes I sound like I have a mouthful of marbles). I've had three or four severe choking episodes where I needed help. I have had the Heimlich maneuver performed to help me get the food up. I've also had one case where I choked and developed aspiration pneumonia.

When I get food stuck halfway down, I have found the most effective solution is to take a tiny sip of noncarbonated liquid to see if it will go down—by gently swallowing several times. I have a cough machine at home. This is like a vacuum cleaner with a hose and mask that fits over your face. As someone holds the mask tight, air is pushed into the lungs, a switch is flipped, and the air is sucked back out. I use the machine mainly to clear excess mucous from my bronchial tubes, and several times it has "saved me" by clearing mucus. This is also very effective when food gets caught because I can use the machine to "vacuum" the blockage up and out.

Eating do's and don'ts:

- Do pay close attention when you eat
- Do eat smaller bites
- Do chew deliberately and longer than usual
- Do have a drink available when eating
- Do try not to eat alone
- Do find the foods that give you trouble and avoid them
- Don't eat while lying down
- Don't talk when eating
- Don't rush; take your time
- Don't try to swallow when laughing

Some foods may cause you more problems than others. Nuts or popcorn, for example, and other small foods tend to get stuck, causing the choking reflex. Some foods are prone to forming clumps that get stuck, such as bananas, french fries, certain types of soft cookies, and so on.

As well, taking large tablets or pills can often present a challenge. Work with your pharmacist to get the best pills possible for you to swallow. Generally, you'll find that taking smaller medications reduces the risk of choking. If possible, get tablets that can be broken up or chewed. It is also helpful to take pills individually, with lots of water or liquid.

It is common for people with swallowing weakness to have poor or insufficient diets. As we age, protein intake is an essential part of our dietary needs that should be slightly increased and maintained. It is advisable to meet with a dietitian to ensure that your overall diet and protein intake are satisfactory. It is easy to take a daily protein drink as a supplement.

In summary, swallowing weakness in IBM is very common and can become a significant issue. Swallowing needs to be monitored, and any problems should be brought to your doctor's attention promptly.

2.1.2 Problems with breathing

The primary muscle of breathing is the diaphragm. Under normal conditions, the diaphragm squeezes and moves down, creating a vacuum in the chest and sucking air into the lungs. In IBM, some weakness of the diaphragm is almost universal, but it is seldom looked for or detected because the symptoms are not obvious (Dardis et al., 2017). In the Shelly (2021) study, diaphragm weakness was diagnosed in 16% of patients, developing some five years after symptom onset.

If the diaphragm is weak, not enough air may be taken into the lungs. You need to breathe *in* enough oxygen and breathe *out* enough carbon dioxide. Generally speaking, patients with IBM do not experience low oxygen levels; low oxygen levels are usually associated with other medical issues, such as COPD, emphysema, pneumonia, and so on.

The cells in the body require oxygen to create energy. Cells get rid of carbon dioxide as a waste product. In patients with IBM with a weak diaphragm, higher than normal carbon dioxide levels build up in the blood, causing chemical changes. This puts stress on the body, in particular the kidneys. The primary symptoms of insufficient respiration are being tired during the daytime and headaches or confusion.

During the day, the diaphragm gets some help breathing from the muscles in the chest. However, at night, your breathing depends solely on the diaphragm. Thus, problems with the diaphragm are usually first noticed at night in what looks like sleep apnea. You tend to wake up often short of breath. Although you may not notice this, if you have a partner, he or she often will.

Breathing is usually assessed using two primary techniques. First, a sleep study is done to monitor the activity of your breathing during sleep. Second, the amount of air, and the strength of your breathing, can be assessed by a machine that charts breathing. You breathe into a tube, and the device records how much air goes in (this simple test is called spirometry). A machine or a blood test can easily measure carbon dioxide levels.

I had pneumonia in April 2008, and I was still having problems and "not feeling right" by September. My general practitioner referred me to a respirologist for respiratory studies. A sleep study was done, and spirometry. I was shocked when I was told that I was only breathing at 30% of normal volumes because I didn't really notice that I had these problems. I was put on a BiPAP machine at night and immediately felt better.

Eventually, my breathing deteriorated to the point where I needed help during the day, and I was given a mouthpiece respirator to go on the back of my wheelchair. This machine has a thin hose that I can hold in my mouth and suck on, to trigger a shot of air (this is ordinary air from the room, I don't need oxygen). I'm using it right now as I write this book. (This is not the same set-up spinal cord patients have—they often have a hose going straight into their throat that stays in place all the time).

I have seen my respiratory doctor every six months for the last ten years. I am an excellent example of someone for whom the proper detection and management of breathing complications can significantly contribute to the quality of one's life. I have been fortunate to find the best doctors I could ask for.

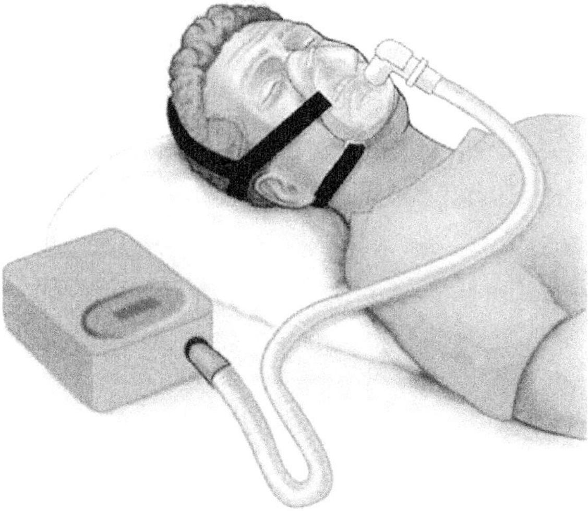

Figure 4 A typical BiPAP machine.

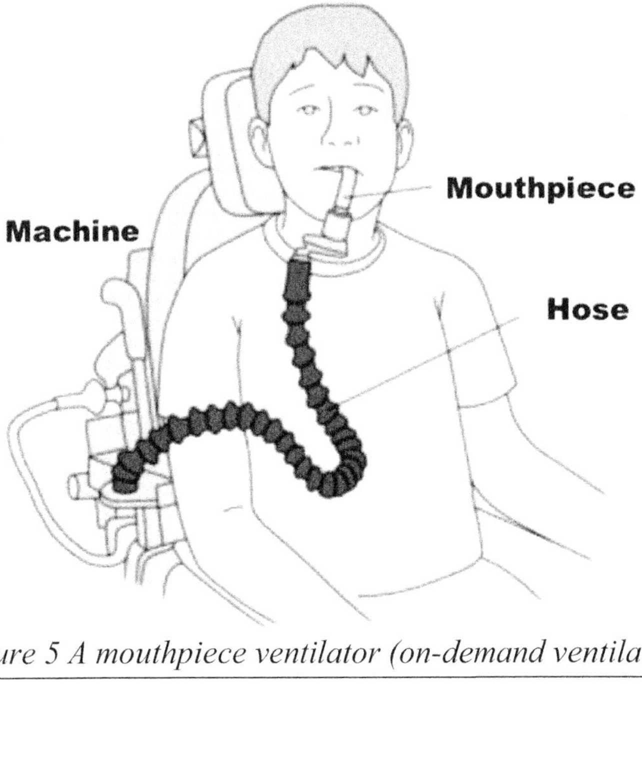

Figure 5 A mouthpiece ventilator (on-demand ventilator

Another common symptom of reduced respiration is a partial collapse of the lung. The lungs do not fully inflate; over time, the tiny air sacs close off and stick together. This usually happens in the bottom parts of the lung. This reduces the amount of air the lungs can use. It also raises the chances of a lung infection or fluid in the lungs (in the collapsed sacs). This partial collapse can be seen in a lung x-ray.

These problems with collapse are common in people with respiratory weakness and are also seen in immobile people who sit hunched over for long periods.

A simple treatment is using a lung volume recruitment (LVR) bag. This device is used to help exercise the lungs and increase the volume of air they can hold. It can also be used to help clear secretions.

Generally, you will need someone to use this device with you. The other person squeezes the bag, forcing air into the lungs and inflating them. Several squeezes may be required for total inflation of the lungs. Your respiratory technician will teach you how to "stack breaths." By holding your breath between each squeeze, you magnify the effect of the bag. This device can be used by patients with diaphragm weakness or in any patient with limited mobility to help keep the lungs healthy. This is something to discuss with your doctor.

> *When I was diagnosed with respiratory problems, an x-ray showed that the bottom one-third of each lung had collapsed. The nurse used an LVR bag to re-inflate them (a bizarre feeling), and now I use "the bag" every morning and evening or when I need to clear excess mucus.*

2.1.3 Problems with mucus

For some reason, patients with IBM often have problems with excess saliva, mucus, and phlegm that build up in the back of the throat and the air tubes leading into the lungs. The mucus/phlegm is usually white and bubbly and can be sticky. This presents significant problems for some patients, and if it is an issue for you, its management should be discussed with your doctor.

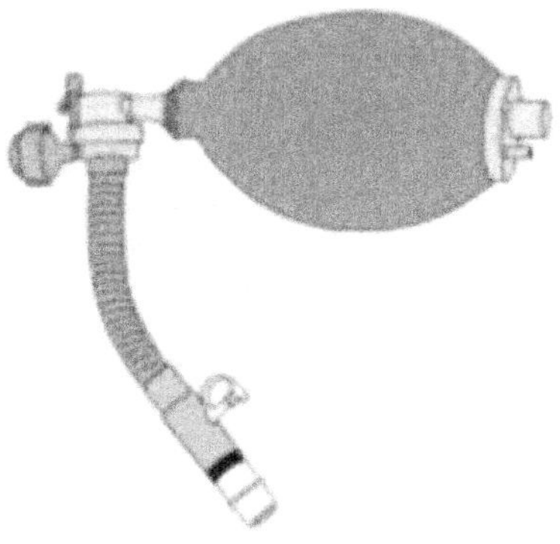

Figure 6 An LVR bag.

In my case, I occasionally have trouble coughing up mucus because, with my weak respiration, it is hard to cough. I had an episode where mucus blocked my breathing, and I had to call the ambulance to go to the hospital; I arrived with a low oxygen level (of 75). It was decided that I should have a cough machine at home.

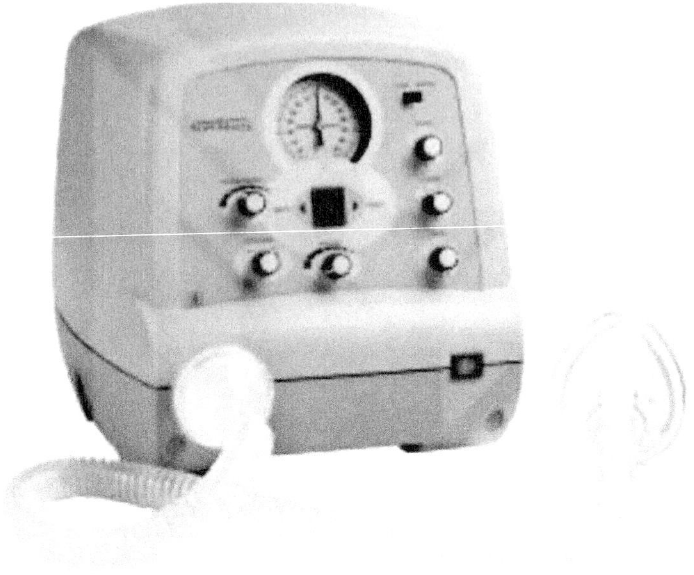

Figure 7 A typical cough machine.

2.1.4 Problems with pain

If you read about IBM, you will rarely see pain mentioned, and many authors have suggested that IBM is a painless condition (e.g., Badrising et al., 2005; Lotz et al., 1989; Pongratz et al., 2004; Sadjadi et al., 2010). This is confusing because many patients with IBM complain of experiencing severe pain. More recent surveys are changing this picture. As we saw above, Keshishian et al. (2018) found muscle pain in approximately 28% of patients with IBM. A study by Bhashyam et al. (2022) found that in a sample of 113 patients with IBM, some 106 (81%) reported pain, and of this group, 88 took pain medication (83%). Of the 88, 55 (62.5%) took opioids, and 82 (93.2%) took non-opioid pain medication.

Pain presents a complex challenge for medicine, and the understanding of pain continues to evolve. Pain was traditionally seen as a symptom of injury. Chronic pain was also understood as a symptom of ongoing injury. When patients reported high pain levels, but no physical cause could be found, doctors often accused them of exaggerating or lying to get prescribed painkillers. Today, it is better understood that chronic pain is a product of multiple factors interacting together (Caneiro et al., 2021; Doleys, 2014; Nelson, 2013). These may include problems with abnormal signals in the nervous system and social factors. How you perceive your pain can also influence how it will impact you (Caneiro et al., 2021). Chronic pain is now seen as a disease process rather than a symptom (Doleys, 2014). Chronic pain is either recurrent or constant, lasting more than three months and often resulting in disability, suffering, or physical disturbance (Urits et al., 2020).

IBM causes significant changes in the muscle. Muscles lose their stretch, and they become brittle. Stretching often causes pain. Squeezing a muscle often causes pain. As well, some patients report having constant pain.

As IBM progresses, our range of motion decreases. Range of motion means how flexible or how bendable our limbs are. It would help if you tried to exercise to maintain as much range of motion as you can while at the same time being careful not to overstretch and rip the muscle. Let pain be your guide; if you are overstretching, it will hurt, so when you feel pain, stop.

The high percentage of patients with IBM treated with opioids (62.5%) reported in the Bhashyam et al. (2022) study is a concern due to the problems often associated with their use. For example, at higher doses, medical complications may occur (poor concentration, depression, drowsiness, anxiety, cardiovascular problems, bowel obstruction, etc.). Accidental overdose can be fatal. Simultaneously using other medications, drugs, or alcohol dramatically increases the risks. Because opioids create "good" feelings, they often become addictive. When you first take the medication, these good feelings are intense but soon disappear, and to achieve these strong feelings again, you must increase the dose you take. Long-term use worsens these problems, and regular usage leads to physical dependence (the body adapts to the drug, and if you stop taking it, you will likely experience unpleasant withdrawal symptoms). The challenge of balancing legitimate medical use of opioids with their risks has long been acknowledged (e.g., Rosenblum et al., 2008). Today, opiates are not considered a first-line treatment for chronic pain (Cohen et al., 2021).

In summary, new research is documenting significant pain associated with having IBM; it will be essential to understand exactly what mechanisms are generating this pain. The answer will lead to a better understanding of managing IBM-associated pain. If you suffer significant pain, you should discuss this with your doctor.

2.1.5 Problems with fatigue

It is common to feel tired, especially if one has had a very active or busy day. Being tired is usually relieved by rest and/or a good night's sleep. On the other hand, fatigue is a more profound and long-lasting feeling of exhaustion and is not relieved by rest or sleep. Fatigue is a day-to-day feeling of weariness that often leads to feelings of depression. Many patients with IBM report feeling ongoing fatigue. If you suffer significant fatigue, you should discuss this with your doctor.

2.2 COMPLICATIONS CAUSED BY LIMITED MOBILITY

Generally, problems with mobility will not come up until your movement is seriously impaired. As we have emphasized above, IBM will impact each person somewhat differently. This often depends upon how old you are when you develop symptoms, how IBM affects you, and how rapidly IBM is advancing.

Many patients with IBM use cannabidiol (CBD) to treat pain. In cannabis, the two main chemicals are CBD (Cannabidiol) and THC. THC is the chemical that gives people the feeling of being "high." CBD is the main chemical thought to help control pain. Cannabis research is very complex because many other chemicals in cannabis could also impact pain. These chemicals also likely interact with endocannabinoids that are naturally found in the body (Anand et al., 2021).

CBD is made from hemp and is supposed to contain only a tiny percentage (.3%) of THC. It can be bought in many forms, usually as an oil or spray, as a food additive, or as "gummies." These products generally do not need a prescription, and their production and sale are not regulated in the United States (they often do not contain what they advertise) (Boyaji et al., 2020; Urits et al., 2020; White, 2019). Research on CBD is complicated because it is often contaminated with THC (and thus it becomes hard to determine which chemical stops the pain). Urits et al. (2020) stated that CBD looks promising for treating chronic pain, but more research needs to be conducted.

Schilling et al. (2020) completed a survey of patients using CBD-related products for pain management, finding that most patients said it worked but wanted more information about CBD, and to get their CBD from their physicians.

To summarize this brief discussion of CBD, the use of CBD for pain is not FDA approved, and there needs to be further research done to validate its use. There are significant challenges in buying CBD that is chemically pure and accurately dosed. Researchers state that it is a promising approach, and patients suggest it works.

You may live your life and not have severe mobility issues. On the other hand, many patients progress to the point where they require a wheelchair and become severely disabled. Studies have suggested that about five years after symptom onset, most patients will need to begin using a cane, and after about ten years, will require a power wheelchair (because of arm weakness in IBM, wheelchairs will invariably need to be powered) (Shelly et al., 2021). Half of the patients in the Shelly study required some walking aid by eight years after symptom onset.

> *I used to have lunch with two IBM friends. One, like me, was in a wheelchair and could not walk. The other gentleman was 75 and could walk without apparent difficulty, although he had trouble cutting his food due to hand weakness. In my case, my disability is considered severe. I can only wiggle my big toes and move my thumb enough to run the mouse on the computer and operate my power wheelchair.*

2.2.1 Swelling in the feet.

When you spend most of the day sitting (either in a stationary chair or a wheelchair), you become vulnerable to developing fluid buildup and swelling in the feet, ankles, and lower legs. This is often called positional or dependent edema (edema means swelling). It is called dependent because the primary cause is sitting with your feet down for long periods. Gravity causes fluid to build up in the tissues. This type of edema is also characterized by pitting and is called "pitting edema." When you press your thumb into the swollen tissue and remove it, it will leave a dent or pit that will take a minute to fill in.

As well as being caused by immobility and sitting with the feet down, muscle weakness in the legs will also contribute to edema. Usually, muscle tone and regular walking motions help keep the fluid in the legs circulating back up towards the body's trunk.

Edema is very difficult to treat and is best managed by prevention. The best prevention is the daily use of compression stockings. These are highly effective. However, the patient with IBM will usually find them very difficult to put on by themselves (it takes strong fingers to put them on).

Chronic edema can become a significant medical issue. First, it can damage the tissues, eventually leading to additional problems. Also, severe edema can squeeze the blood vessels and block the blood flow to the feet; in some cases, gangrene can result.

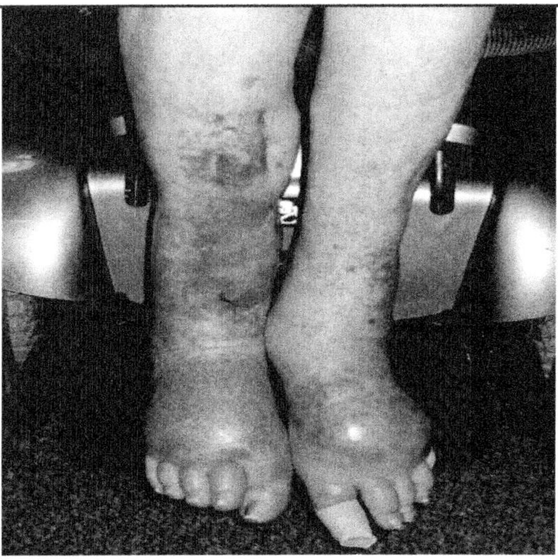

Figure 8 Severe unmanaged edema in a patient with IBM.

Edema is also associated with diet, especially salt, and curtailing salt intake is essential in controlling swelling.

If you have edema, you need to discuss it with your doctor and caregivers in terms of how to help prevent and manage it.

2.2.2 Weight gain

A common mobility-related problem is weight gain. Usually, as we become less and less active, it is human nature to continue eating as we were before. Doing less but eating the same amount leads to weight gain. Ideally, you should reduce your food intake as you lose mobility.

Weight gain is a problem because it puts more strain on weak muscles. It is also related to several potential health issues, such as diabetes and cardiovascular problems.

An IBM diet? People often ask if there is a diet that will help reduce the symptoms of IBM. It is fair to say that a good, healthy diet should suffice. It is common to see diets advertised that will "help cure" various medical problems. Research has not shown a diet to specifically help people with IBM.

2.2.3 Skin problems

As we age, the skin naturally tends to become thinner and more prone to injury. These problems are magnified by the loss of mobility.

Limited movement is commonly associated with pressure-related skin problems. Long periods of pressure on a small spot restrict the blood supply. This often results in skin breakdown, blisters, or open sores. "Pressure sores" are usually caused by people sitting or lying in one position for long periods; the force of gravity pushing straight down creates pressure. Common areas where these sores occur are on the heels, the inner surface of the knee, the buttocks, the hip (on the side of the leg), and the elbows and shoulders. Once the skin has broken, it can be slow to heal, and ulceration may occur. Sadly, pressure sores are a significant cause of death from infection, especially in the elderly.

Patients in wheelchairs usually use specialized air cushions to help minimize the development of pressure sores on the buttocks. Patients with IBM often have difficulty turning over in bed, increasing the likelihood of pressure sores. As we will see in the next chapter, a specialized mattress may help.

Another way skin problems can develop quickly is through shear. This is caused when friction puts pressure on the skin. As illustrated in the example shown in Figure 9, the skin on the buttocks is being held in place by the friction of the bed but is being pushed down by gravity. When this happens, the skin is distorted and quickly develops a blister to start; if this is not addressed, an open sore may develop. Hospital beds that raise the head also raise the knees simultaneously, preventing this shear from developing on the buttocks.

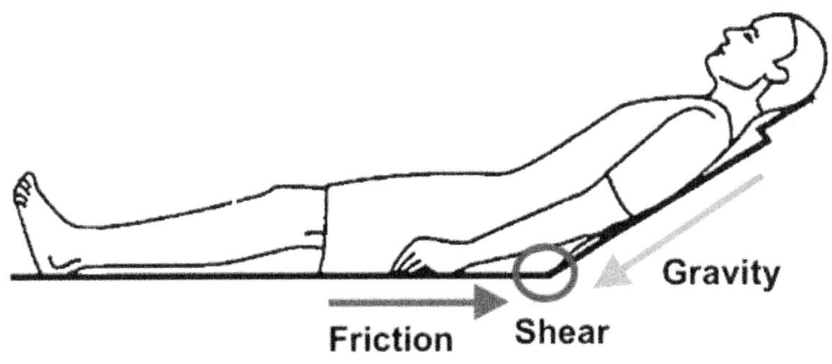

Figure 9 Skin shear.

Skin likes to be clean and dry. Problems quickly arise when skin is moist for long periods, especially with poor hygiene. Sweating and being contaminated with urine or feces quickly irritates the skin and causes a rash. The cleaner and dryer skin is, especially in the groin area, the better.

I have found that it is better not to wear underwear; I wear oversized sweatpants that give some extra room, helping to avoid moisture and overheating. I have also found that I seem cold without normal muscles, so I wear warm tops.

2.2.4 Bowel issues

Normal motions associated with walking help keep bowel movements regular. People with compromised mobility and who need to use a wheelchair often find constipation a problem. Generally, it helps to keep your fluid intake high, and a daily laxative may be indicated. This should be discussed with your doctor.

2.3 COMPLICATIONS: KEY POINTS

- Weakness in swallowing is a common complication.
- Breathing weakness may occur.
- Excess mucus is common.
- Pain is a common complication.
- Many patients complain of chronic exhaustion.
- Lack of mobility may cause complications: skin breakdown, swelling, and weight gain.

CHAPTER 3: DIAGNOSIS AND TREATMENT

3.1 DIAGNOSIS

In general, diagnosing any disease involving muscles is considered a challenge. Because most muscle conditions impact your life so much, a correct diagnosis is critical.

IBM is considered a challenging disease to diagnose, partly because it is an extremely rare disease and many physicians are unfamiliar with it. It is not unusual for patients to see several doctors and have more than one biopsy to arrive at a diagnosis. On average, it takes about five years for a patient to receive a diagnosis of IBM, and from 40% to 53% of cases are initially misdiagnosed (Goyal & Mozaffar, 2021; Greenberg, 2019).

Another reason IBM is hard to diagnose is that the symptoms of IBM vary widely from person to person. There is no one "textbook" presentation, and the symptoms often depend upon how far the illness has advanced when the doctor sees you.

Diagnosis begins with a patient going to the doctor, usually complaining of weakness. It is common for the patient to be told that they are "Out of shape and should try to exercise more." Occasionally, the doctor may attribute your situation to aging. For example, in one case, the doctor turned to the spouse and asked if the patient "Was having problems with depression from not being able to deal with the expected declines associated with aging."

When problems are recognized, your family physician will usually refer you to a specialist, either a rheumatologist or a neurologist. The first step is to have a careful physical examination done. The doctor looks for the signs of weakness and makes an assessment. The doctor also asks about your history and symptoms.

The exact pattern of weakness usually seen in IBM is quite specific.

When doctors examine you, they will test the strength of your muscles, for example, by asking you to push against their hand. In this way, doctors can determine if muscles are weak in "the typical IBM pattern" (the muscles responsible for flexing the elbow, wrist, and fingers, elbow and knee extenders, and ankle dorsiflexion). Because IBM is a rare disease, it is helpful to see a doctor with experience diagnosing it in other patients.

> *I met an expert in IBM, Dr. King Engel, at a conference. He spent about five minutes talking to me and said, "I suspect you have IBM." I asked why and he said, "I could feel the weakness in your hand when we shook hands." He invited me to his clinic in Los Angeles for a proper examination; that is where I had my third biopsy and diagnosis.*

Antibodies are chemicals in the immune system that help the body recognize and fight off infections. In autoimmune disorders, autoantibodies recognize normal body parts and begin to attack them. The discovery of autoantibodies in the blood of patients with muscle disorders has been a significant step forward in understanding and diagnosing these various muscle diseases. Different autoantibodies have been linked to different muscle diseases.

An autoantibody called anti-cN1A has been discovered in the blood of patients with IBM, and it was hoped that this could help in the diagnosis of IBM. Unfortunately, only about 50% of patients with IBM have this antibody. If you have been tested and have this antibody, you likely have IBM; however, if you do not have it, you may or may not have IBM. Therefore, this is of limited use in diagnosis. The discovery of this antibody supports the idea that IBM is an autoimmune disorder.

Usually, a series of tests is conducted. Routine tests include a blood test looking for chemicals that indicate muscle damage. An examination of the electrical activity of the nerve, called a nerve conduction study (NCS or NCV), is usually done. This test involves placing electrodes on the skin and mildly stimulating the nerves to check their functionality.

A muscle test (called an EMG) will likely be conducted. In an EMG, thin needles (like acupuncture needles) are placed in the muscle, and electrical activity is recorded, looking for abnormalities.

When I had my EMG done, I was watching the computer panel. It had a bunch of squares that should have all turned green if the test results had been normal. By the end of my test, every square on the computer screen was red.

Usually, your doctor will want your muscle looked at under the microscope. This process involves a biopsy: taking a small piece of muscle (about the size of a sugar cube), usually from the arm or thigh, and sending it to a laboratory. This procedure involves minor outpatient surgery and afterward can be pretty uncomfortable for the first day or two.

Finally, doctors may want to conduct genetic studies of your blood, looking for genetic markers that may indicate a higher-than-average likelihood of developing IBM.

It is not unusual to see several different specialists who have different opinions. One strategy many patients use is that once a diagnosis of IBM is mentioned but not confirmed, they will seek out the closest facility and specialist having experience with IBM. This information is usually obtained from searching the Internet.

In my case, my first biopsy was inconclusive, and the doctor said: "Because there is no treatment for any of these muscle diseases, you shouldn't worry about the diagnosis." I asked for a second biopsy, and, again, it was inconclusive. Finally, I had a third biopsy, and the diagnosis was made.

Because IBM takes so long to diagnose, it is often a very frustrating experience, and it takes a great deal of patience. Generally speaking, it is essential to follow the process to its end and arrive at a diagnosis. A specific diagnosis allows you to learn about the disease you have and better understand its impact on you. It also enables you to see what treatment or management options are available. You and your family need to be strong and consistent advocates in the diagnostic process.

It is helpful to have a list of questions to take to the doctor, and it is also beneficial to have someone with you. It is common to be overwhelmed with information and have difficulty remembering everything the doctor has said.

IBM and ALS look similar in the early stages, and IBM is often misdiagnosed as ALS (see sidebar). It is also common for doctors to misdiagnose patients with IBM with a similar-looking disease called polymyositis. This illness comes on very quickly, over weeks or months, compared to IBM, which comes on over months or years. As well, polymyositis usually responds quite well to medication. If you have been diagnosed with polymyositis and have not responded to medication, the doctors will often review their diagnosis and change it to IBM.

In summary, IBM is a frustrating and challenging disease to diagnose, both for doctors and patients. The diagnostic experience is often quite variable and depends on factors like your age, how weak your muscles have become, what part of the world you live in, and the experience level of the doctors you see. It also depends on being calm and consistently advocating for yourself.

When talking to people about IBM, what they often "hear" is that you have multiple sclerosis. IBM is also often initially misdiagnosed by doctors as ALS. Here are four conditions that can be confusing to keep straight.

First, let us look at Alzheimer's disease (AD). In Alzheimer's, abnormal protein clumps similar to those seen in IBM form. However, in IBM, abnormal proteins appear *inside* the muscle cells; in Alzheimer's, the abnormal protein accumulates *between* nerve cells. That is a huge difference. Alzheimer's causes the nerve cells in the brain to die, leading to loss of memory and thinking skills, eventually leading to death.

Another disease of the nerves that involves abnormal proteins is Parkinson's. Parkinson's usually affects people over the age of 60 and causes tremors (shakiness) in the muscles and other movement abnormalities.

Sometimes people confuse IBM with multiple sclerosis (MS). Nerves have insulation, like the insulation on an extension cord. In multiple sclerosis, an inflammatory attack breaks down the insulation of nerves of the central nervous system—the brain and the spinal cord (not the nerves of the peripheral nervous system). This damage impairs the electrical transmission of the nerve signal, and over time this leads to problems controlling muscles and other issues.

Finally, some patients with IBM are first mistakenly diagnosed with amyotrophic lateral sclerosis (ALS). ALS is difficult to diagnose in its early stages, and the muscle weakness is easily mistaken for IBM and vice versa. ALS affects the brain and the nerves of the spinal cord. It is invariably fatal, leading to death some five years after diagnosis. The disease is associated with Lou Gehrig, a famous baseball player who developed it.

To emphasize, IBM *only* affects muscles and does not impact the nerves or the brain.

When I was told it was likely that I had a muscular disease that would be chronic and progressive, I had to accept the idea that I would have this disease for the rest of my life. Therefore, I decided the best approach would be to look at this as a "professional patient." From now on, it is my job to be a patient, and I need to do a good job. I will be the continuous thread as I age and see different doctors over time. I need to understand the illness as well as I can and what problems it may cause so that I can watch for them.

Learning about the disease was a shock and made me sad at first, but I took the approach that it was my responsibility to look after myself the best I could, with the help of my family, my caregivers, and my doctors.

3.2 TREATMENT.

Today, in 2022, no medication is recommended as a standard treatment for IBM and research has not shown any medication to be effective. Over the years, many different types of medications designed for other diseases have been tried, but none has been shown to slow down or stop IBM. It is a challenge for researchers to develop a new treatment for a disease when the primary cause is unknown.

Sometimes, doctors will prescribe a treatment "to see how it works." It's important to realize that medications often have significant side effects. It was once common for doctors to try prescribing anti-inflammatory drugs to patients with IBM. This made sense at the time because IBM shows inflammation of the muscle tissues, and these medications are designed to treat inflammation. A recent study showed that some 44% of patients with IBM were treated with corticosteroids (often prednisone) (Naddaf et al., 2021). This is somewhat surprising as research and experience now show that corticosteroids do not help, have very unpleasant side effects, and can be challenging to stop taking.

"There is no evidence that treatment with corticosteroids has any benefit in patients with IBM, and thus it should be avoided" (Naddaf et al., 2021, p. 7).

When my first biopsy came back ambiguous, I asked for a second. The doctor said, "Why don't you go on Imuran [an immunosuppressant] for a year and see what happens?" My reply was, "Wouldn't I want a diagnosis first?" He said, "A year on Imuran won't hurt you." I declined and went on to my second biopsy.

Treatments may be used in patients who have IBM-related side effects. For example, patients with diaphragm weakness often need help breathing, especially at night; effective treatment is using a BiPAP machine.

Patients with severe problems swallowing will sometimes be given treatments—sometimes medications, and sometimes a procedure done to the muscles in the throat. These are very specialized treatments for those who routinely choke and can no longer eat safely.

"No medication" does not mean "do nothing." For example, occupational therapy, exercise, and physical therapy are now recommended. It used to be thought that exercise would only speed up weakness and should be avoided. Today, it is highly recommended to find a physical/occupational therapist or a fitness trainer to work with.

It will likely be hard to find a therapist with knowledge of IBM. However, many therapists are certified to work with patients who have debilitating conditions (like multiple sclerosis or Parkinson's). Please work with your medical team to find a therapist and help them design a unique exercise program for you to address your current situation.

When I first went to the doctor (some twenty years ago), the advice was not to exercise because it would damage the muscles.

> A specialized exercise called blood flow restriction (BFR) is being researched for muscle diseases, including IBM (Jørgensen et al., 2022). In this technique, the muscle's blood supply is restricted while exercising, usually using some type of tourniquet. This may turn out to be an effective way for patients with muscle diseases to exercise.

Generally speaking, muscles that IBM already impacts should not be exercised, but it now seems that it is advisable and helpful to exercise healthy muscle. The Myositis Medical Advisory Board of The Myositis Association recommends using high repetition, low-intensity, low-impact exercise and slowly increasing duration and intensity to mild resistance exercises. See the links to "Exercise and Physical Therapy" and "Exercise in Place" in Chapter 7.

Some exercise programs are conducted in a saltwater pool; the water creates buoyancy that takes the weight off your legs. As with all exercise, you must be careful not to overdo it.

I spent about twenty minutes in a hospital saltwater pool. I walked back and forth with water up to my neck, holding onto a rope going across the pool. It felt wonderful because I had not had the experience of walking "normally" for a long time, and in the water, I felt free. When I returned to the house, I could barely get from the car to the door using my rollator. My legs were completely exhausted.

In summary, there is no recognized, approved medication that will slow or stop IBM. Hopefully, treatments will emerge as more is discovered about IBM. A specially designed exercise program often helps. Patients having complications from IBM may require specialized equipment or treatments. Generally speaking, it is a challenge to accept the idea that such a debilitating illness has no treatment. Unfortunately, it does not appear that treatment is "on the horizon." Patients usually benefit from learning about IBM, counseling, and emotional support, both for themselves and their families and caregivers.

3.2.1 IBM checklist

Once IBM has been diagnosed, it is generally helpful to have objective measures of how it is progressing and impacting the patient. It isn't easy to measure the impact of IBM. When you ask people questions, they often have difficulty estimating how strong or weak they are. When given treatments, this is especially true: people often report feeling stronger, but actual physical measurements show no change.

Despite these problems, researchers have developed checklists for IBM. One checklist to help measure mobility, the IBMFRS-9, divides function into the upper body and lower body (Ramdharry et al., 2019). The section on the upper body covers the ability to write, cut one's food and feed oneself, do fine motor tasks, dress, and perform routine hygiene. Included in the lower body items are: turning over in bed, the ability to stand up from a chair, the ability to walk, and the ability to climb stairs. Swallowing/choking is included as a separate item.

3.2.2 "No treatment" may be a recipe for desperation

Patients should avoid falling prey to unrecognized or unproven treatment approaches. Many patients often have trouble accepting that no medication can reverse or help this illness. It's common for patients to feel desperate and to try to find cures themselves. For example, patients often look to the possibility of treating IBM with stem cell therapy. Stem cell therapy is a prevalent idea on the Internet, and many companies advertise these services, often in foreign countries. Unfortunately, while stem cell therapy holds great promise, it has not been developed to the point where it can help patients today. Here's what the FDA says about stem cell therapy in the United States: "Stem cells have been called everything from cure-alls to miracle treatments. But don't believe the hype. Some unscrupulous providers offer stem cell products that are both unapproved and unproven" (FDA, 2019). Some patients go to foreign countries where stem cell treatments are not regulated. This exposes them to unknown risks. In the future, stem cells will likely be part of the solution in treating IBM—but not today.

Today, at the end of 2022, there is no stem cell treatment available that will help IBM. Work is being done to develop muscle stem cells, and there is a possibility in the future that this will be successful. It is unclear if the muscles damaged by IBM will be able to integrate new muscle stem cells and produce new muscle tissue that will be functional. The link for more information is provided in Chapter 7.

Many supplements and "special formulas" are promoted for just about every disease imaginable. Various products are advertised as good for building healthy cells and muscles. These products may not be harmful, but there is generally no research showing they are of any benefit. Generally, these products are costly and are often sold by subscription. As always, your doctor is likely the best person to give you advice on the advisability of any sort of supplement.

3.2.3 Finding "your" doctor and when to go

When you have a chronic condition like IBM, it is essential to find a general physician to work with who can follow your case as problems arise. You need proper ongoing assessment and referrals to specialists when necessary. It is also essential to know when to reach out to your doctor.

In general, go to the doctor when:

- You have a fever lasting more than 24 hours.
- You have trouble breathing or are short of breath.
- You have suicidal thoughts.
- You suffer severe chest or abdominal pain.
- You choke, and a couple of days later, you cough up colored material.
- Your phlegm turns color: yellow, green, or brown (it should be white).
- You have difficulty peeing, or if it hurts when you pee, or if you have to pee a lot, if your pee is very dark, has blood in it, or smells bad.
- Your poop is black or has blood in it.
- You have fallen and struck your head.
- You have problems with memory or confusion.
- You feel lightheaded or dizzy, especially after standing up quickly.
- You feel depressed for more than ten days.
- You have diarrhea that lasts more than three days.
- There is swelling in the ankles or legs.

3.3 DIAGNOSIS AND TREATMENT: KEY POINTS

- IBM is a challenging disease to diagnose.
- No single test will prove or disprove a diagnosis of IBM.
- In about 40% to 50% of cases, a misdiagnosis is initially made.
- On average, it takes five years to reccive a diagnosis.

- Usually, a biopsy is required to make a diagnosis.
- Diagnosis relies on the expertise of the doctor.
- The doctor has to look at several things, including the clinical presentation: which muscles are weak, and a combination of other factors, including biopsy, imaging, laboratory results, antibodies, and EMG.
- Many indicators (protein aggregates, rimmed vacuoles, Anti-cN1A antibodies, etc.) are not always present in every case.
- No treatment has been developed for IBM.
- The use of corticosteroids is no longer recommended.
- Complications may require treatment.
- Patients need to be aware of fake or false treatments.
- Having a good relationship with your primary care doctor, who can follow your progress and make referrals when necessary, is critical.

CHAPTER 4: CAUSES AND RESEARCH

IBM was first named in 1971, and since then research has been ongoing all over the world. Although it is a rare disease, it is the most common acquired muscle disease seen in patients over 50.

We can safely say that muscle research, in general, is a challenge. Muscle is a complex tissue, and it is not yet fully understood how healthy muscle functions.

4.1 OVERVIEW OF CAUSES

Today, in 2022, the primary cause of IBM has not been discovered. It is clear that this is a very complex illness, and it seems that it is probably caused by more than one factor. Over the past fifty years, several theories of what causes IBM have been proposed.

When researchers first looked at IBM-impacted muscle, it was apparent that there was degeneration of muscle tissue: cells in the muscle were being killed, and the muscle was shrinking. Many abnormal proteins were found clumped together in "inclusion bodies" in the muscle cells. This led to the theory that IBM is a "protein aggregate disease."

Later, in 1984, researchers saw that the immune system attacks the muscle cells in IBM. Why would an autoimmune response occur? Under normal conditions, the immune system should see healthy muscle cells as part of the body and not attack them. However, in some situations, an autoimmune disorder can arise where the immune system mistakenly sees part of the body as a problem—the same way the immune system sees an infection or a virus in the body and attacks. A typical example of an autoimmune disorder is rheumatoid arthritis.

As we described above, one of the most prominent findings in IBM

Evidence that IBM is a type of autoimmune disease is strong. It includes predisposing genetic risk factors, many cells within IBM muscle tissue that secrete antibodies, and the frequent occurrence of Anti-cN1A antibodies in the blood of patients with IBM. Researchers see cells from the immune system (CD8+ T cells) surround, invade and kill muscle cells in IBM muscle. These killer cells are multiplied in the muscle tissue and are found in both blood and multiple muscles in patients with IBM. These cells display a "flag" on their surface researchers called KLRG1. All muscle cells show over-activation of MHC - I antigens, indicating an autoimmune cascade. The idea is that these cells are attacking a target (an auto-antigen) that has not been discovered. This attack goes on for years. For some reason that is not understood, in IBM, immunosuppressive medications that generally should help in this situation do not work (see Lundberg et al., 2021). Based on the work of Dr. Steven Greenberg, a company (Abcuro Inc.) has developed a medicine to attack and kill these invading cells. Research is going on today to develop and test this approach.

is inflammation of the muscle cells. Inflammation is the first reaction triggered by the immune system when it senses something wrong (e.g., the presence of a virus, bacteria, infection, etc.). Inflammation is designed to heal and protect the body, but chronic inflammation becomes part of the problem in cases of autoimmune disease.

Cells need energy to function. There are structures called mitochondria in the cell that provide the necessary energy cells require. These mitochondria have also been discovered to have significant problems in the muscles impacted by IBM. Mitochondrial abnormalities are part of the degenerative theory and are another factor that needs to be accounted for and explained.

Another early theory was that a virus infects the muscle, causing

IBM, but no virus has been reliably linked to IBM.

Of course, it is also possible that some undiscovered cause is a trigger for IBM that sets off the problems they've already discovered. Time will tell.

Why do some people get IBM and others don't? Part of the answer is that it appears there is a genetic predisposition to getting IBM. As explained above, if you happen to have a particular combination of genes, it is more likely that you will develop IBM than people who do not have those genes.

People often ask whether they got IBM from their job. For example, working in specific industries often exposes people to various chemicals—like working in an auto body shop or a factory. At this point, there has not been any kind of environmental trigger, like a chemical, identified.

In summary, today, researchers know that several things are going wrong in the muscle cells that IBM impacts. Just exactly what the initial trigger is and how IBM develops remains a mystery. It is fair to say that over the last twenty or thirty years, the autoimmune and the degenerative theories have been the two "front runners," and each theory has attracted much research. The autoimmune component seems prominent, but how the different pieces fit together is not yet clear. More years of study will likely be needed to discover the fundamental cause of IBM.

4.2 RESEARCH

4.2.1 Muscle: A general overview

Muscles are very complex and have been researched for years. There are two basic types of muscle—striated and smooth muscle. Striated muscle has long, thin parallel streaks or stripes and includes

> Recently, the results of a significant study were reported showing that some 99.5% of multiple sclerosis (MS) patients have Epstein-Barr virus infection. This is complicated because 94% of healthy individuals also have Epstein-Barr virus. This study was done on over 10 million people who had served in the United States military (Bjornevik et al., 2022). Research has shown that the immune system attacks the Epstein-Barr virus but that the Epstein-Barr target (EBNA1) is similar to a myelin sheath protein (GlialCAM). Sometimes, a cross-reaction occurs, and the immune system mistakenly targets the myelin sheath protein, causing MS symptoms (Lanz et al., 2022). Two questions arise. What factors play a role in triggering this cross-reaction leading to the development of MS? Second, could the same sort of mechanism be going on in IBM, and if so, what are the factors involved?

the skeletal muscle and the cardiac muscle (the heart). Smooth muscle is characterized by layers and is located inside organs, such as the stomach, blood vessels, and intestines.

As a side note, it can be confusing when you read about muscles because we talk about "muscle cells," but these are also called "muscle fibers"—each muscle fiber constitutes a muscle cell. Muscle tissue is full of blood vessels, has many nerves connected to it, is infused with lymphatic vessels, and plays an important role in circulating the lymphatic fluid in the body. About 80% of muscle is made out of proteins and uses chemical energy (ultimately from what we eat) as its energy source.

Usually, the ends of skeletal muscles attach to tendons; in turn, tendons attach to the bones. When stimulated by a nerve, the bundles of muscle fibers pull their ends together and get thicker. This causes the muscles to pull on the tendons (no muscle in the body can push). The muscular and skeletal system is designed using a series of levers to create the necessary movements we need to survive.

Generally, roughly 650 muscles account for approximately 40% of total body weight. Muscle fibers work together to provide the force necessary to move. As muscles work, they need a constant influx of oxygen and nutrients from the blood, and they continually release waste products, primarily carbon dioxide and water.

Muscles are subject to wear and tear as they are used—the proteins involved in generating muscular energy often break down during exertion. After muscles are used, they rest, and during this time, they are repaired, and new muscle is generated. After vigorous exercise—more than you are routinely used to, more new muscle is generally created than damaged. This makes the muscles get larger as we exercise. This creates a problem because we will not function efficiently if the muscles become too big. While exercise increases muscle size, a chemical (myostatin) stops muscle growth, thereby maintaining a balance in muscle size.

Healthy muscle is designed to be constantly used. When muscles are not used, for example, when confined to bed, they rapidly begin to shrink (atrophy). After long periods of disuse, muscles must be slowly strengthened and rehabilitated. As well, IBM also causes affected muscles to shrink from being damaged.

> If IBM has no specific treatment, could we increase muscle growth by slowing down the effect of myostatin? And would this help counterbalance our damaged muscles? This has been researched in patients with IBM and found safe; however, it has not improved strength (see Schmidt, 2019). This would be a good approach until a specific treatment is discovered, and hopefully more research will lead to better results in the future.

4.2.2 Research focused on IBM

The research focused on IBM looks at the problems in the muscle fibers and what may cause them. As described above, research has explored several avenues over the years, with some laboratories looking at muscle degeneration and abnormal proteins and other researchers looking at the immune system response or other issues, like the role of mitochondria. Unfortunately, it is common to see research produce results that are open to interpretation but that often suggest avenues for further study. Studies are often hard to generalize because they sometimes report a case study of one person or, more often, only a handful of cases (the 2021 study by Shelly et al. involved a case review of 21 patients; ideally, you would like at least a few hundred cases, if not more).

Research goes on very slowly, and "breakthroughs" are few and far between. Today, researchers continue to look for existing medications or new drugs that may help patients but not knowing what causes IBM makes this process much more challenging. When a fundamental cause has been determined, generating a specific treatment should be easier. Once an IBM treatment looks effective in preliminary research, it still has to go through rigorous clinical trials and will take many years to become widely available to patients.

In summary, research continues to try to find the primary cause of IBM. Understanding what causes IBM will help researchers zero in on effective treatment. This research has gone on for some fifty years and actively continues today.

4.3 CAUSES AND RESEARCH: KEY POINTS

- IBM likely has multiple causes.
- No cause has been discovered.
- There are two main theories: autoimmune disease or a degenerative process.
- Research is actively ongoing.

CHAPTER 5: PHYSICAL ADAPTATION AND MANAGEMENT

As mentioned above, one of the frustrations of having IBM is that it is a constantly moving target—you are continually, slowly, getting weaker and weaker, and your functions and abilities change accordingly. The adaptation you make that helps today may not work in six months or a year from now. Generally, it is helpful to understand "where the disease may go" and prepare/plan for the future. This chapter will highlight some of the significant issues that commonly arise.

5.1 COMMON MOBILITY TERMS

You may be asked about your mobility during your journey, and it is essential to understand a few basic terms. Can you transfer? There are four significant types of transfers:

- On and off a toilet.
- In and out of bed.
- Getting up from a chair.
- Getting in and out of a vehicle.

Do you need assistance to do these transfers? Some people need a lift to get in and out of bed or to use a wheelchair. There are various types of lifts, some portable and some fixed to the ceiling.

Another common question concerns how ambulatory you are:

- How well can you walk?
- Do you fall frequently?
- Do you require a cane or walker (rollator)?

Your ability to climb stairs is often included in how ambulatory you are.

- Do you have to take each stair individually?
- Do you require assistance from someone else?
- If you do fall, can you get back up by yourself?
- Do you find it challenging to step up onto a standard curb?

Can you toilet independently and attend to proper hygiene, or do you need assistance toileting? Many people find it upsetting to contemplate needing help in the bathroom: remember, the priority has to be staying safe and maintaining good hygiene and health.

In assessing physical function, it is common to talk about "activities of daily living." These are the normal activities needed to care for oneself independently and usually include being able to:

- Perform daily personal hygiene.
- Control urine and bowel function.
- Dress oneself.
- Feed oneself.
- Get in and out of bed.
- Walk and climb stairs.

5.2 THE HIGH COSTS OF ASSISTIVE EQUIPMENT

To have a chronic disability is expensive. The more disabled you are, the more associated expenses you will have. In considering financial impacts, one must also factor in lost income for those who cannot continue working full time or who must give up their jobs. Assistive equipment is diverse and expensive. There are also high costs if home renovations are necessary. Finally, there are significant costs related to transportation and receiving extra caregiver help, if required.

5.3 THE MOBILITY EQUIPMENT JUNGLE

Experience quickly teaches us that equipment for the mobility challenged is confusing, and patients often face the additional challenge of unscrupulous sales practices. This is a huge business, and it is a business first. Often customers are directed towards sale products that are unsuitable for their needs; a typical example can be seen at the front of most stores where affordable, but often inappropriate, scooters are on sale. This is undoubtedly an area of "buyer beware."

Unfortunately, many people end up purchasing equipment that isn't right them. Thus, you need to be careful. Equipment must be appropriate for your size and weight and the function it will serve. Generally, you need advice from experts like occupational therapists—not salespeople—to get what you need. Another point: once you know what you need, a good option may be to look for used equipment.

There is a tremendous variety of equipment designed for mobility, from canes to walkers, some without wheels, some with (rollators), to all different kinds of wheelchairs.

I started with a spring-loaded hiking/walking stick. I used a metal cane before I progressed to a rollator. Eventually, I started falling on my rollator and decided I would have to get a wheelchair. My first wheelchair ended up with 5000 miles on it. I'm now in my third wheelchair. I would say that I should have moved to a wheelchair sooner than I did.

Terminology around assistive equipment is confusing. Generally, a walker is a device to give you stability, and you need to carry/push it forward as you walk. A rollator also gives you stability while walking; it has four wheels, usually with handbrakes and a seat. Because patients with IBM have weak arms, a standard manual wheelchair will not work. You need a power wheelchair if you are going to drive it yourself.

Usually, a power wheelchair has a more adjustable seat to tilt, recline and raise your feet.

A scooter is usually designed for portability (many fold up) and more temporary applications. Some have three wheels (quite unstable). As a rule of thumb, if you're in a chair for long periods, you will need a proper power wheelchair. The drawback is that they are much more expensive.

Figure 10 A walker A rollator

Figure 11

A 3 wheel scooter scooter power wheelchair

5.4 TECHNOLOGY IS OUR FRIEND

We are fortunate to live in times where technology can be of practical help in living life and getting things done. For example, many online programs (or apps) are available to order meals, groceries, and all kinds of merchandise without leaving your home. Several voice-activated virtual assistants are available that can answer questions, make calls, and carry out commands by simply speaking to them. Paper maps have become obsolete now that your destination can be entered into an application on a cell phone, and a voice will tell you where to turn. Finally, modifications to a computer can make it easier to use when you lose finger dexterity. Changes may include using a different mouse and specialized software like an on-screen keyboard and a voice recognition program. I am writing this book using speech software.

Many people are intimidated by technology. There are significant benefits to learning even a few simple programs that you can use on your cell phone or computer. There are likely courses available in your community for seniors to learn about these technologies. Anything that makes life easier is welcome when challenged by a movement disorder.

5.5 PROBLEM AREAS IN THE TYPICAL HOUSE

Equipment is designed for specific problems faced in a home environment. The stores are full of equipment for the bathroom, including the bathtub and toilet. There are many different kinds of lifts available, some portable, some designed to be installed in the house.

The Yale IBM survey found that some 95% of patients with IBM live in a residential home, either their own or a relative's house. Often, high costs are associated with adapting your environment to your needs—for example, modifications to bathrooms or the addition of ramps or elevators.

It is essential to understand that modifications are designed to create a safe environment for individuals whose mobility is challenged. Many falls and injuries are associated with people trying to "get by" in a standard setting. The correct assistive equipment and modifications prevent injuries and allow safe access, especially to bathrooms and bedrooms.

There are two common scenarios. First, you may do renovations on an existing house. Depending upon the house's configuration, this can be easy or impossible. Consulting an expert is usually worthwhile, and many communities have associations that provide advice. Second, mobility enhancements can be part of the design when building new—for example, the placement of an elevator and appropriate ramps.

You may find it challenging to prepare meals for yourself in the kitchen. There are many specialized kitchen utensils and appliances that are designed to help those who have limited finger dexterity. You may eventually find it difficult to cut your food or to be able to feed yourself.

The bathroom and bedroom are the two most dangerous areas in the house. A wide range of specialized accessories are available for the bathroom to help those with mobility challenges. In the bathroom, using the sink may become difficult or eventually impossible. Getting on and off the toilet may become challenging or impossible. Generally, it is challenging (and likely dangerous) to use a bathtub when the strength in your arms and legs is compromised. A roll-in shower, in combination with a shower/toileting chair, is preferable. This type of chair can roll into a shower and over the toilet.

Getting stuck on a toilet, sliding off, and getting stuck between the toilet and the wall, are all-too-common experiences for people with IBM. (In the early stages, if you are using the bathroom independently, it's a good idea to have a cell phone with you in case you have trouble).

Unfortunately, most hotels are not well adapted for people who need assistance. You may find yourself, as I did, in a hotel where you get stuck on a low toilet and cannot get up. In my case, they had a telephone beside the toilet. After 20 minutes of trying to get up, I had to call. I explained the situation and asked if they had someone who could come up and help me. Sometimes you just have to accept the situation you find yourself in and ask for help.

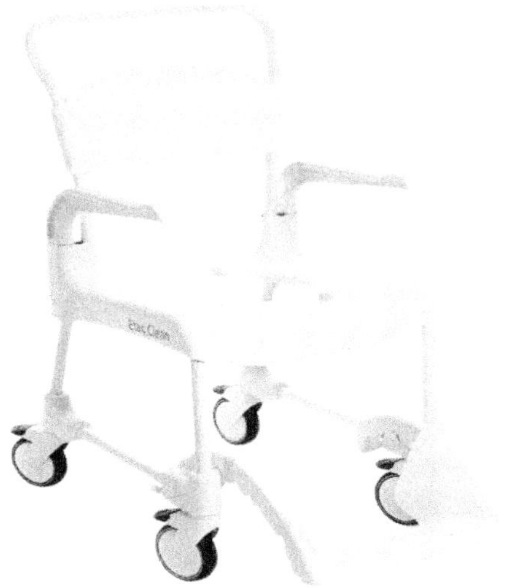

Figure 12 A typical shower/commode chair.

Getting in and out of bed can be difficult, and falls often occur around the bed. Depending on your ability to turn over in bed, you may need some sort of cushioning mattress (like the air mattresses used in hospitals). Many doctors and patients recommend using a hospital bed to raise and lower the head. Elevating your head (at about 20%) helps prevent lung problems in persons with limited mobility.

As I became weaker and weaker, I found it more and more challenging to get comfortable in bed. Using a so-called "memory foam mattress" made things worse because I got stuck and could not move at all. I used a gel top mattress, which was successful for several years. Finally, I had to get a hospital bed with a medical air mattress. This mattress automatically adjusts itself, pumping in air to match my body's pressure and contour.

I would also mention that I used to approach the bed in my wheelchair to transfer (before I had a lift). On one occasion, I caught my sleeve on my control stick and essentially ran myself into the side of the bed, compressing my feet under the bed. (This is a common type of scenario with your power knob, and you have to be very attentive, especially when driving by stairways.) I now transfer with a ceiling lift.

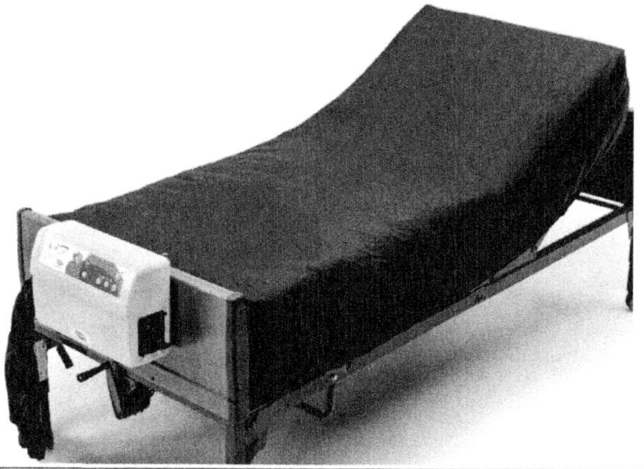

Figure 13 A typical hospital air mattress and bed.

Other common problem areas involve doorways that have a raised door sill (such as the front door or a backdoor), stairways, and uneven sidewalks, pathways, and lawns.

5.6 PROBLEMS WITH TRANSPORTATION

Many patients with IBM must come to grips with having their ability to drive a vehicle threatened or come to an end. The ability to steer and brake can be impacted by weakness in the arms and legs, and sound judgment needs to be exercised. Safety over pride should be kept in mind when making decisions about your ability to drive.

For those in a wheelchair, using a modified van (driven by someone else) may be necessary to maintain independence. Generally speaking, the modification of a van adds some $25,000 to the original (new) price.

At first, I used an ordinary van. I had a near-fatal incident when I was driving. I went to put my foot on the brakes as I approached a yellow light. My leg did not lift, and instead, my foot went sideways from the gas pedal under the brake pedal. Then, I found my foot stuck under the pedal and unable to stop, and I had to hit the gas and rush through the light as it turned red. This was a very eye-opening and frightening experience that helped me decide to switch to hand controls.

I used hand controls for about 18 months until my arm strength gave out. Since then, I've been a passenger in a regular wheelchair-adapted van. There are two main types; in one style, you go in the back; in the other, you enter through the side—this is the kind I have. I have an automatic lock on the floor to hold my wheelchair stable, and I sit beside the driver.

5.7 EXTRA HELP.

One of the realities of IBM is that most patients eventually have their daily activities severely curtailed. In many cases, you need extra help to live a basic life. You need to consider what care you need and who will provide it. In most cases, initially, these additional duties fall on the shoulders of your partner or family. As discussed in Chapter 6, family and loved ones often find themselves severely stressed and burned out.

It may be necessary to arrange professional (hired) caregivers who can help you. Many caregivers live with the person they are looking after.

5.8 ALTERNATIVE HOUSING

It may be the case that you cannot live on your own. You may need to explore alternative housing solutions like an "assisted care facility" that can offer you a safe environment and meet your care needs. Depending upon where you live, there may be programs to help you meet your needs financially.

You need to explore the resources available in your community, find and talk to the people responsible for dispensing resources, and take advantage of the programs that may apply to you. Your doctor or occupational therapist should help you access these services in most cases.

5.9 PHYSICAL ADAPTATION: KEY POINTS

- Mobility aids are costly, and you need good advice before buying.
- Because you continue to weaken, a forward-looking view must be taken in planning.
- The vast majority of patients with IBM live in private residences.
- Modifications are designed to create a safe environment.
- Most accidents occur in the bathroom or bedroom.
- Most cases will require assistance from professional caregivers.

CHAPTER 6: PSYCHOLOGICAL ASPECTS OF COPING

IBM is a physical illness, but it has a significant psychological impact on you as a person, as well as on your family, co-workers, and friends. This chapter will discuss some psychological challenges involved in dealing with a chronic and progressive disorder. Why is this important? Because it can help you help yourself.

When I say psychology, what do I mean? Who we are reflects our psychology—our deep values and attitudes forming our unique personality. Personality represents your particular way of thinking, feeling, and behaving, making you a unique individual with your own way of seeing and interpreting the world. Personality develops over time and is influenced by genetics, learning, experience, the beliefs you create, your faith, and the environment you grow up in. IBM challenges your "old self" in many ways, but it is important also to realize that our personality will make a big difference in how we see and deal with IBM. It's important to realize that your personality is not set in stone, and you can influence and shape your personality. For example, you can shape your values and views as you gain experience and learn more about life—and IBM.

How can I change? I don't know anything about psychology! In my experience, many people go through life without realizing that they can play a significant role in creating who they are. So, why don't people realize this? Because they are not aware. If I am standing on your foot and unaware of it, I won't do anything about it. But, as soon as I notice, I can move my foot and apologize. Becoming aware is the first step that allows you to evaluate yourself. Are you overly negative? Pessimistic?

Do you have unrealistic expectations? All these things can be examined, and if you find the need to change, then you can think about what changes you need to make.

Having IBM will likely change your goals and priorities in life. Old goals may have to yield to new ones. As you begin to get used to the idea that you have IBM, you will go through many ups and downs regarding your emotions and your thinking. Over time how you see yourself will likely change.

Change is often triggered by major life crises. Major crises disrupt our smooth, day-to-day routines and force us to take a hard look at ourselves. Becoming ill is such a life event. But this also has a silver lining in that we can become aware and discover ourselves and draw on new resources and new perspectives. Some may encounter new perspectives that are bleak, depressing, and disturbing. Some may feel that they have reached the end of the road. On the other hand, with an open mind, awareness can bring you new opportunities and discoveries about yourself. It is said that character emerges when faced with adversity. Adversity does not create one's character; it uncovers it.

> *I have been fortunate to have had two lives; one, learning about people and myself as a psychologist. I didn't expect to fall ill, but when I did, I discovered my second life by learning about my new illness and how to help myself and others cope with it.*

How you see the world will impact how you see IBM and approach it. Each of us will come to know this illness uniquely; we will react

"If you don't like something, change it.
If you can't change it, change your attitude."
Maya Angelou

differently and cope with it individually. There is no one way to feel or think about the discovery that you have an illness like IBM. There is no right or wrong way to feel. As emphasized above, if you are open to discovery and take advantage of new opportunities, these changes can be positive and lead you to a deeper and more satisfying appreciation of life.

Summary.

- IBM will challenge and change our old view of ourselves.
- The impact of IBM is unique for each of us.
- People uniquely experience their illness.
- People uniquely react to their condition.
- People learn how to cope uniquely.
- How we see IBM will affect how it impacts our lives.
- Becoming aware of ourselves allows us to examine and shape who we are.
- One major aspect we can control is our attitude.

6.1 THREE PHASES

I have found it useful to think about the three phases of becoming ill with IBM. The first phase is before diagnosis—we realize we have problems but haven't yet sought out a doctor. The second phase begins when we see a doctor and the diagnostic process begins. The third phase begins when we receive an IBM diagnosis. Each phase presents unique psychological challenges.

6.1.1 The first phase: before diagnosis

The first phase begins when we notice symptoms—we see that there is something wrong. Often, this phase is prolonged because the signs come on very slowly and are mild at first. Thus, we don't immediately seek a doctor. Because we don't know what's wrong, this phase is characterized by anxiety, uncertainty, and ambivalence. Ambivalence means that we go back and forth in our mind from feeling something really serious is wrong (this causes anxiety) to the other extreme—that we are okay and just making too much out of our symptoms. In this initial phase of uncertainty, it's easy to catastrophize and think the worst (this seems like a natural human tendency for many people).

At first, IBM tends to be an "invisible" disease. You have problems that you don't understand and which others don't see. Your friends don't realize why you're not walking up the stairs as fast as they are or why you're always taking the elevator. It's frustrating to explain that you have problems, only to have people look at you blankly. I had several people say, "What's wrong with you?" That's a difficult question to answer when you don't know what's wrong. It can also be hard for partners and families to understand your challenges.

The phase before the diagnosis is often a frightening and confusing time. The symptoms are initially subtle, yet they are undoubtedly real and get your attention. Tripping and falling out of the blue is frightening, and there's a great deal of anxiety over not knowing what's wrong.

One positive thing about this early phase is that symptoms are coming on very slowly, and you have time to adjust. It would have been quite a different situation if I had had an accident, broke my back, and woke up the next day paralyzed.

6.1.2 The formal diagnostic process begins.

Once you do seek medical attention, the process of diagnosis begins. Generally, the more serious an illness, the more critical it is to achieve an accurate diagnosis. As I've emphasized, IBM is one of the most challenging muscle diagnoses to make, and this is shown by how long it takes the average patient—five years. Looking at it from the patient's point of view, five years is a long time not to know what you have. You must be strong and advocate for yourself as you go from doctor to doctor and have one test after another. Be strong, be professional, and don't take setbacks personally. This is important to get right, and you must play your part.

When we first approach doctors, we are often met with skepticism because diseases causing weakness are rare. Usually, when doctors see weakness, it reflects being out of shape, and they will first recommend exercise.

I was forty, fairly heavy, and clearly out of shape when I first approached the doctor. When I complained of weakness in my arms and legs, the doctor suggested working out. There was an exercise area at my place of employment. For four months, I worked out under the supervision of trainers. After four months, I had made no progress in strengthening myself, and I was told that this was unusual.

One night, I had trouble getting out of the bathtub, and the next day, I called the doctor's office back. I was seen at the neuromuscular clinic. When it was my turn, I had trouble getting out of the chair, and the nurse said, "What's wrong with you?" My reply was: "That's what I'm here to find out."

This first phase is also challenging because there is a natural and understandable fear of what could be wrong. On the one hand, you want to know, but on the other hand, you know there's something seriously wrong, and you're afraid.

My neurologist offhandedly said it was either a muscle disease or ALS, and he sent me to a rheumatologist. I knew what ALS implied; that was certainly a difficult three weeks of anxiety waiting for the appointment. I saw the rheumatologist with my blood test of 2000 (CK), and she said dismissively, "I see people with 200,000; I'm sending you back to the neurologist for more muscle tests."

Diagnosis is a time of frustration and confusion. The following points will guide you through the process.

- It is challenging to diagnose IBM.
- All muscle diseases are challenging to diagnose.
- Experience has shown that an IBM diagnosis is not a straightforward and smooth process.
- Many disorders have very similar early symptoms, and many people are initially misdiagnosed (often as polymyositis).
- This is usually a long, frustrating, and difficult process.
- Often, a patient is sent to a specialized clinic or hospital for diagnosis and testing.
- Some clinics also research IBM.
- There are two significant aspects to a diagnosis:
    - Clinical: Doctors examine us and ask questions.
    - Tests: Blood tests, special tests, biopsy, etc.
- When facing any major illness, it is wise to get a second opinion on the clinical aspects and the test results.

Many doctors may have many opinions.

- Patients often must see a confusing series of doctors.
- Most patients start with their family doctor and are referred to a specialist.
- Some patients will see a rheumatologist, some will be referred to a neurologist, and many will see both.
- Different types of doctors will approach us from different perspectives based on their training.
- Seeing multiple doctors can be frustrating: each may have a

different idea about what's wrong and what to do about it.
- Two doctors may make a different diagnosis, often with the same confidence.
- It can be challenging to deal with different opinions and recommendations.

We need to be heard.

- "I'm not crazy . . . and I'm not just lazy." I use this quote for a reason: because sometimes people are initially "put off" by doctors as "imagining things" as "being lazy" or as simply "getting old."
- Try not to get emotional: always focus on the facts.
- You know your symptoms and when something is wrong, no matter how strange it sounds.
- Sometimes, describing precisely what you feel is wrong is hard.

Diagnostic roadblocks.

- It seems that many people encounter various "roadblocks" in getting their diagnosis.
- Diagnosis is a complex mixture of evidence and the doctor's experience, attitudes, and intuition.
- Don't take setbacks personally; try to be professional.
- Consistently return attention to the questions, evidence, and issues important in weighing your particular case.
- Many patients with IBM go through similar experiences—talking to them will help you deal with frustrations and empower you to get an accurate diagnosis.

Hard questions.

- You will likely have to make choices in diagnosis.

- Should I ask to have a second opinion?
- Should I have that extra expensive test done?
- What if the doctor suggests I try a treatment? Management options? Try a clinical trial?
- Doctors will summarize information and choices; however, the patient must make the final decisions.
- We may need a "crash course" on IBM to be able to know what to do.
- We often need help understanding some of these choices.

6.1.3 Diagnosis—now what?

Once we receive an IBM diagnosis, we enter a long phase of slow physical and psychological adaptations. I find it helpful to divide this phase into five major areas.

6.1.3.1 Personal

You must come to grips with the fact that you are ill and will have to change your lifestyle significantly. Whatever other support you have, this boils down to a personal and private coping process. Part of coping is accepting and seeing change as positive. Not only change in function or your environment, but change within yourself.

With an illness with no medical treatment, coping becomes paramount, and the one thing we can control—our attitude—makes a huge difference in how we move forward. Despite the significant challenges of this disease, a good, positive attitude makes a big difference. If you are a person of faith, do not abandon your beliefs—you need your faith more than ever now.

You need to reach out. Talking to other patients with IBM who have been "in your shoes" can often help you. A significant part of coming to grips is realizing that the future is partly what you make it. Reach out for counseling; do not push away those who love you. Use their love and support for strength.

When I went to university, I had a professor whom I liked. He used to say, "We often must deal with things in life that we would not have chosen, but, as challenging as these things are, it could always be worse." I remember these words and take heart that however challenging I find the situation—I can always be thankful that I didn't have ALS or have something else worse than IBM.

Summary.

- We alone must face up to the fact that we are ill, that our life and lifestyle will likely change.
- Whether you are alone or have family support, this is a personal and private process.
- Others can help us, but ultimately, we must "come to grips with it" on our terms.
- How we see our illness is critical to our subsequent attitude, which is essential to how we will react and cope over the long term.
- Coming to grips is a process that occurs in bits and pieces over time.

6.1.3.2 Family impacts

For most people, families are a significant source of support and strength. If you have a partner, IBM will significantly impact them. If they had come to know you before IBM came along, the changes you are enduring will change your relationship. These changes do not have to be negative. With good communication and realistic planning, your relationship can become stronger in facing challenges.

As you can do less and less, your partner and family have to do more and more. Don't forget, your partner likely had "a full plate" before you fell ill, and all these additional jobs add to their existing load. This often puts a tremendous strain on your partner. You need to recognize that your partner can only do so much.

Roles are an essential part of the family structure that are often challenged when IBM enters the picture. Remember your primary role; you are, for example, a husband or wife, a father or mother. Don't let your "job" as a patient with IBM take over from your usual role in your family's structure. And if your partner needs to help as a caregiver, do not let either of you lose sight of your primary roles. For example, a wife who is a caregiver is a wife and mother first. No one should be "demoted" to the role of caregiver in a way that diminishes who they are in life. You married your partner; do not demote them to the role of caregiver.

Respect is always critical in dealing with relationships, more so than ever when dealing with a challenge like IBM. Good communication and realistic expectations are needed to ensure that the help given by your partner and family does not create burnout for them. You need to monitor both your health (physical and mental) and that of your loved ones. This situation needs to be seen as a marathon race. Good planning for the family who acts as caregivers must include building in regular rest periods and bringing in extra help when needed.

Family: As you go, so they go.

- Families are often sources of strength for us.
- Our illness/symptoms directly impact those who love us: spouses, parents, and children.
- Spouses often experience many of the factors mentioned here, but their reactions often go unrecognized.
- The "patient" and the family should be seen as a unit; neither

exists in isolation from the other.

Family: Spouse acting as a caregiver.

- Spouses often must take on new caregiver roles, a unique, complex, and very demanding task.
- As your function becomes limited, your spouse must do more, but they can only do so much.
- If your spouse is your primary caregiver, the extra tasks may eventually become too much.
- Burnout is physical and psychological exhaustion.
- Recognition and prevention of burnout are critical.
- Once burnout occurs, it is tough to recover.
- Good communication is vital.
- You both need to plan for the long term, often, eventually, needing to bring in extra help.
- Built-in, regular rest periods for spousal caregivers need to be scheduled.

But what if I'm alone? A chronic disease like IBM is difficult to cope with at the best of times, but if you do not have the benefit of family support or you are on your own, it may become overwhelming.

- Many of us will be dealing with IBM alone, with no spouse or family support.
- Being alone will make it harder to stay positive and to be motivated to look after yourself.
- It's easy to get stuck in negative thinking and give up when alone.
- When alone, reaching out to other patients with IBM in support groups can be critical support.
- Your doctors need to know you are alone and how you feel.

6.1.3.3 Community Support

No one can understand your situation better than someone else "in the same boat." This is where the "IBM community" may be able to help. I've always found other patients with IBM to be a welcoming and strong source of support.

There are several non-profit patient organizations that offer services, support, and research funding for the worldwide myositis community. In the U.S., for example, Myositis Support and Understanding (MSU) and The Myositis Association (TMA), offer an array of IBM support groups on their community platforms, supplemented by monthly support sessions. Wherever you are in your journey and wherever you are in the world, there is a support group for you. Check Chapter 7 for links to patient organizations and support groups whose services you might benefit from.

6.1.3.4 Dealing with doctors

Because IBM is a chronic illness, you will be dealing with doctors for the rest of your life. You need to have a good relationship with doctors you are comfortable with. You need to find the right doctors for you. Generally, this applies to both a primary care physician (family doctor) and a specialist.

In dealing with chronic and untreatable diseases, the concern, understanding, and compassion of your doctor will become significant factors. A surgeon can take out your appendix regardless of their attitude toward you. But IBM is a different story, and you need a doctor who cares and is concerned about your overall welfare, including your attitude and psychological adjustment.

Few family doctors know much about IBM, and many will appreciate your role in helping them learn. Having a supportive medical team will help you cope as things move forward.

Depending on your case, your medical team may include: a family doctor, a neurologist (a doctor specializing in the brain, the spinal cord, nerves, and muscles), a rheumatologist (a doctor specializing in diseases of the joints, rheumatic diseases [autoimmune and inflammatory diseases], muscles, and bones), a respirologist (a doctor dealing with respiratory issues), a physiatrist (a doctor dealing with physical problems and rehabilitation), a dietician, a dermatologist (a doctor dealing with skin), a physiotherapist, a respiratory technician, a speech therapist, an occupational therapist, pharmacist, and a psychologist or social worker. It may be helpful for you to look at yourself as part of this medical team: you will play the role of a good patient.

In 2016, I had a sudden episode of low blood pressure (50/40) that put me in intensive care for five days. It turned out I had a pulmonary embolism. On the second day, I had 13 people attend me, and I joked with one doctor that if I saw a gynecologist, I would have seen every type of doctor in the hospital.

Summary

- Our medical team is a major, ongoing part of coping; finding the right team for you is critical.
- The team's care, compassion, and advice are vital, especially in "untreatable" conditions like IBM.
- Feeling that the team is there and understands is an essential support for the patient.
- Doctors "know" about illnesses but don't have the "wisdom" gained from experiencing them.
- Doctor's tools: caring, compassion, and science.
- Doctors help give us a context for our illness—the "big picture."

6.1.3.5 Social relations

If you had a broken leg, crutches, and a cast, your coworkers and friends would immediately understand your situation. But as we said above, IBM is not an apparent illness. It is not evident that anything at all is wrong with you, to begin with. As you learn about IBM, you often have to teach others about it. Educating ourselves about IBM helps us be able to inform others, and ultimately this helps us cope. Telling our story repeatedly—sometimes until we are tired of hearing it—helps us hear our story ourselves, which in turn helps us stay realistic. As mentioned above, sometimes friends will not deal with our illness and will leave.

On the other hand, you may have friends who become overly helpful. They may go to great pains to share their ideas about "treatments that you should try," and sometimes they can be insistent. Unfortunately, it can be hard to explain that there is no accepted treatment, and you want to "stick with the science."

Summary

- "But you don't look SICK." It is hard for our extended family, friends, and co-workers to understand our illness.
- IBM is not obvious to others—not like a broken leg.
- Our illness may impact others in unexpected ways—friends may leave.
- We need to educate others about IBM.
- We have to tell "our story" repeatedly, but in telling others, we also help ourselves cope and face reality.
- Overly "helpful" friends may be a problem: everyone seems to have advice or a "solution."

6.1.3.6 Relations with professional caregivers

We talked above about creating a physical structure that would act as a safety net in your navigation of everyday functions. Here, we discuss creating a safety net consisting of a supportive and sustainable infrastructure of caregivers. What do I mean by sustainable? A network that won't break down over time, one that spreads the load and is resilient to stress.

What is an "infrastructure"? It's just an organization of parts—in this case, people, usually family and professional caregivers. When a person progresses to the point when they can no longer help themselves with day-to-day functions, it is usually the case that caregivers have to be hired.

There are many different types of organizations that provide care. This varies tremendously depending on your location. Ideally, you will find the resources you need and the funding to pay for them. Some agencies provide help by the hour. Some full-time caregivers come into your home for one shift at a time. Some full-time caregivers live with you in your home.

> *As I became weaker and weaker, I first used caregivers from an agency who came to see me five days a week, in the morning. This was a bit chaotic because, generally, different caregivers would come every day. They didn't know me or my needs, and I had to explain everything repeatedly.*
>
> *I was fortunate to secure a series of live-in caregivers. Today, Rene has been with me for ten years, Joey for five years, and Nancy for three years. My wife and I feel lucky to have these three nurses looking after me and to have their families be part of our family.*

6.2 LEARNING ABOUT IBM

It is a significant challenge to be told that you have a disease that most people have never heard of (including doctors). There are substantial advantages to learning all you can learn about IBM, especially the symptoms and implications.

Imagine yourself falling (as I did), squishing your ankle, and ending up in an emergency room. The nurse asks you if you have any medical conditions, and you say, "Yes, I have inclusion body myositis." She looks at you blankly. She asks you if you are on any medication, and you reply that you are. You say that you are on an antacid and allopurinol. She recognizes that—it's a medication for gout. She smiles. The doctor comes in, and she says to him, "This patient has gout and injured his ankle." If they don't understand what you say, they often won't ask—and your information about IBM won't get passed on. Now, this is where you have to tell the doctor that you have IBM. The chances are that you will be the one explaining to him what this is and its implications.

> *I did a lot of research as part of my job before I got sick, so it was relatively easy for me to become very familiar with the research on IBM once I was diagnosed. On one visit to my neurologist, I had the newest article in my hand while waiting, and the nurse noticed. She came over, looked at it, and commented, "Don't read that stuff. You'll get confused; just do what the doctor says."*

There is a lot of information available on IBM—too much and too complex to be of any practical use to the average person. On the other hand, it is beneficial to have a broad understanding of the basic facts. People have their comfort level of knowledge regarding how much they want to know. Find your comfort level. Always use your judgment to consider the source of information regarding its credibility and reliability.

Types of information.

- Personal/Family: Many types of information can help us develop insight and the strength we need to face and manage this illness.
- Medical: Medicine is like a foreign language.
    - How much do we need to learn to "get by" to understand and talk to the doctor about the diagnosis and our management options?
- Information helps us effectively give others a context to understand our situation and the unique challenges we face.

Levels of information.

- How much do you need to know?
- Set your balance: don't be afraid to learn, but don't feel forced to learn more than you want to.
- General information on coping with a chronic illness, disability, and living a good life ("self-help").
- Specific information about IBM.
    - Information is written for a general audience.
    - Experts write information; very specific and complex.
- A wide variety of all types and levels of information is readily available today.
- Patient groups, our medical team, the Internet, books, and various not-for-profit associations.

Information and support.

- Seek out an IBM support group (see Chapter 7).

- Most people struggling with IBM face many of the same challenges as you do.
- Talk to others about their experiences and their challenges. How THEY cope may give you ideas about how YOU can manage (and inspire you).
- Other people are a great source of information, practical advice, and emotional support. Don't be afraid to talk to people about IBM.
- The best approach is a balance of information we learn and our practical experiences.
- Coping involves practical experience we learn from living with IBM.
- Practical knowledge we can learn from other people we talk to is also essential.
- Remember: Take it one step at a time and take your time, "learn as you live."

6.3 GENERAL ASPECTS

All muscle diseases share in common that they disrupt the normal activities we have come to take for granted. IBM is also a challenging illness because it is progressive. Its impact is minor to begin with, but as the disease progresses, the impacts accumulate and increase. Depending upon the specific situation, the impairment may also be minor or major, and the degree of impairment at any given time makes a great difference to the patient.

6.3.1 Abilities and opportunities

There are three main aspects to understand when we talk about abilities. The first involves exactly how IBM will impact us—as we explore below, we have no control over this. The second aspect involves how other people see us; again, we have no control over this aspect. Finally, there is the aspect of how we see ourselves, and we have significant control over this.

In many cases, people have no understanding of mobility issues and can be very cruel in how they see us and what they say.

Once I was sitting in my power wheelchair in a slow-moving line. I heard someone in the back say, "Oh, there's a cripple in the line holding things up."

We cannot be responsible for the ignorance of others. On the other hand, we *can* control how we see ourselves. You may be very different than you were before, but, as in my case, you may still be very able to do things—different things, perhaps, but still important things.

How you see yourself is crucial, and you need to know how you define your abilities. Many people focus on what they have lost, not what they can still do. If you only focus on what you can't do, you will lose sight of what you can. Abilities change as we age. Abilities change as IBM weakens our muscles, but we can still be happy and contribute positively with the right attitude and a focus on what we can do.

It is important to remember that when things change, some doors will close. You may not be able to stop doors from closing, but when they do, look for new doors to open and new things you can do. For each activity you must cut back on, look for a new one to begin.

Our lives will change more than the average person's, and it is a challenge for us to cope with change and keep moving forward, even if it is not on the original path we had in mind for ourselves. We need to become experts at changing, adapting, and coping.

I was working half-time for about a year while waiting for my diagnosis. When I got my diagnosis, I told my supervisor. He said, "Don't worry, we have people on the job who have multiple sclerosis." I said no, "I have inclusion body myositis, it is a type of muscular dystrophy," and I was on long-term disability illness the next day. I was shocked, and my overall feeling was, "What am I going to do now?" I was surprised because I immediately started volunteering and have never been busier over the past twenty years since that day. I've looked for opportunities and have been able to take them and give my life a new meaning—one that I hadn't anticipated but one that has become important for me.

In summary, we must see change as a series of new opportunities. We need to see opportunities as chances to learn and contribute to new things. What you cannot control, try to adapt to. Be clear about the things you cannot change versus those under your control. Once again, our attitude plays a critical role in adapting, seeing our abilities, and discovering and seizing new opportunities.

6.3.2 Juggling life challenges

There is no one impact of IBM; therefore, the life challenges that IBM presents are largely unique to each person who has IBM. But there is no question that as function and abilities are impacted, it becomes harder to juggle doing everyday tasks. When it's easy to do things, we often don't plan very well and do things one at a time. For example, we will take three trips to get the groceries, pick up the grandkids in school, and mail that parcel. Impacted ability calls for multitasking. This means doing two or more things (tasks) at once. To do this effectively, we must adapt and make ourselves more efficient, disciplined, and organized. It takes concentration and mental discipline to multitask. It also takes practice. Here, I will talk about multitasking to help deal with IBM.

Having IBM makes doing ordinary things difficult. Think about running to the store for a quart of milk. What used to take you fifteen minutes may now take you an hour. Planning and prioritizing tasks and grouping things together make life a lot easier. For example, when buying groceries, plan and list things you need and only go to the store twice a week.

Set realistic goals and time frames. You can't do ten things a day anymore. Unfortunately, you may have to limit yourself to one or two essential things every day. Why? With IBM, it boils down to a question of practicality and energy. Doing things with IBM takes much more energy, and you have to pace yourself—using your energy tires you out. Add in extra time based on your level of mobility. Add in spare time to get organized and dressed appropriately to go out. Add time for your helpers to get ready. When things take additional time, it's essential to reduce redundancy. You don't have time to go out twice, so you must make one trip count.

Great planning is an excellent defense against the stress and chaos of limited movement. Plan both your days and your week ahead. If you can't get it done today, don't get stressed—have it in your mind to be flexible, and what you can't do today, add to your next trip.

Being organized and multitasking will help. But expectations are also critically important. Don't expect to do things the way you used to. Expect that it will take much longer and require more effort to do less. For example, getting up and going to bed become projects. Getting in and out of the bathroom or shower needs a routine and more time. Eating (or being fed) now takes much longer.

Many basic tasks also become more challenging to accomplish. In many cases, to do something, you have to explain it to the person helping you, which can be challenging both for you and them. You lose significant control when you become dependent upon others. A simple example: you often rely on others to get things for you and to put things away, so you may have no idea where those items actually are. Two of my most common statements are "Where is that?" and, "I have one of those somewhere." Again, patience is a critical element every day.

I have found it helpful to consider balancing three things that can help us organize our activities. First, we need to differentiate between activities that we will be doing in the house (which don't require transportation) versus jobs we need to do when going out (appointments, shopping, etc.). Second, we have to look at things we can do ourselves (for example, me working on the computer) versus things we need help doing. Last, we can pay attention to the connection between time management and managing activities by clearly understanding what we need and want to do and how long it will take. Then, we need to plan and schedule these activities with this timeframe in mind.

In summary, doing basic tasks takes longer, is more challenging, and takes more energy when you have IBM. Excellent planning and efficiency in multitasking help, along with reasonable timeframes and expectations.

Multi-management

- A muscular illness challenges us to organize and manage our lives more effectively.
- There are many different aspects to living life, and most are affected by IBM.
- Coping involves learning how to manage many aspects of life with a chronic illness.
- What do you have to do to make these steps successful? IBM calls on us to be excellent life managers.
- Everything we do takes longer, is more complex, and uses much more energy.
- Great planning is our best defense.
- Progressive movement disorders call for ongoing adaptations: e.g., house modifications and transportation.

- We need to increase efficiency, reduce redundancy, and generally be very well organized in all we do.
- Several aspects require a dual focus.
    - Activities in the house/activities when going out.
    - What we can do ourselves / where we need help.

6.3.3 Lifestyle choices

During our lives, we make many choices about what to do every day. Often, these choices don't significantly impact our overall life. On the other hand, some of our picks are more important in determining our future.

I'm going to look at our health as a teeter-totter—on one end, we have health, and on the other, we have an illness.

Figure 14 The health and illness teeter-totter.

The healthy end is up in the air for most people, and the illness end is down. We have to do our best to emphasize positive practices that contribute to health and minimize harmful factors to our health (this is especially true as we get older).

What are the factors that tilt the teeter-totter up and down? First, we have genetics—we are born with certain genetic predispositions to make us more likely to develop certain illnesses or protect us from getting certain diseases. Then we have the environment we are exposed to. For example, many people who live in big cities are exposed to high levels of pollution that impact their health—the immune system and breathing, for example. Finally, we have our choices: our diet, how we handle stress, our social network (that exposes us to both support and conflict), and our use of alcohol and drugs, including nicotine.

Our ability to make positive and healthy life choices becomes more critical when dealing with a chronic illness.

When a chronic illness impacts you, it becomes essential not to make problems worse by making bad choices, because the balance is already tipped. If you have issues with weight, smoking, or drugs, it is important to discuss this with your doctor and get their advice and help.

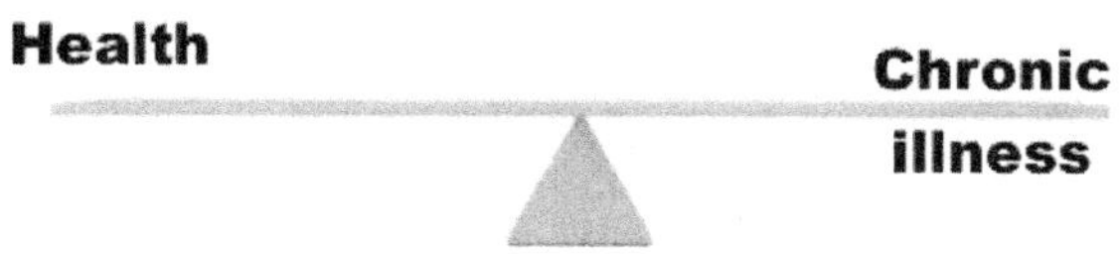

Figure 15 The chronic illness teeter-totter.

My family doctor retired, and I found a great new one. He asked if I had any other problems, and I said, "Apple pie," and we laughed. But it is no joke; it is difficult to control your diet while struggling with something like IBM.

Important lifestyle choices boil down to your goals. What is your overall goal? Is it to focus only on today? Or, is it to maximize your health by making some difficult choices today to focus on the long-term? Only you can answer these questions in making your choices. We each face unique decisions, depending on our situation and goals. Try to make choices with your health in mind.

Major lifestyle choices.

- Life, health, and stress management often involve many lifestyle choices and changes, and often major and very hard decisions.
    - Stop smoking, lose weight, reduce alcohol, etc.
- People with chronic disorders need to put these changes into the context of their illness.
- Balance and weigh changes against our goals.
- What is our central goal in making complex changes?
    - To maximize our quality of life.
- The choices we each face will differ depending on our situation: we must try to make positive changes to improve life.

Health management.

- Many factors contribute to our overall health.
- Genetic factors.
- Environment: what we do, all that is around us.
- Social: psychological and emotional well-being, stress, support network (family, friends, medical team, psychologists).
- Diet: amount & type of food, hydration, exercise.
- Nicotine, alcohol usage, and all kinds of drug usage.
- We must be very aware of our overall health status—and "health quotient."
- We must develop positive practices and minimize factors harmful to our overall health.

6.3.4 Fatigue

I touched on fatigue in Chapter 2, but I will mention it again. One of IBM's most common and intense impacts is ongoing mental and physical exhaustion, sometimes leading to fatigue. As mentioned above, fatigue is a feeling of exhaustion that does not recover from periods of rest—it is a feeling of being burned out that requires awareness and attention. Once you reach the level of fatigue, it is often difficult to recover without help.

Fatigue is a complex problem because it has both physical and psychological aspects. When you feel weak, it takes more energy to do daily tasks, and the physical elements of IBM are very tiring. But the mental stress associated with the changes IBM brings also contributes to feeling tired. Chronic fatigue impacts how we feel, think, and behave and is often a component of depression.

The physical and psychological aspects also interact—overdoing it physically may lead to both mental and physical exhaustion.

> *In 2000, I was still using a cane, and I went to a conference. It was on a high hill, and the hotel was at the top. On the first day, I walked up the hill. I underestimated how far and how steep it was, and by the time I got to the top, I was completely exhausted. I could barely move the next day, and I had to take the hotel's golf cart. That was a good lesson in learning to pace myself.*

Points to consider.

- patients with IBM often feel very tired all the time.
- May lead to fatigue/burnout—more serious.
- Fatigue: reduced motivation and energy.
- Tiredness can sometimes cause depression or may be a symptom of depression.

- Overactivity can lead to several days of exhaustion and slow energy recovery.
- Energy needs to be considered ahead of time when planning activities.
- Do not plan too many activities in one day.
- If you overdo it, stop and let yourself recover.

6.4 PSYCHOLOGICAL ASPECTS

I will explore twelve general and basic ideas about the psychological challenges of dealing with a chronic disease like IBM. I will avoid giving much specific advice, because everybody's situation is different, but I will outline a few things to think about and what to look for.

It's common for people to have problems and not realize how severe they are. If you find yourself reading this and acknowledging that you need help with something, please seek help. This is a complex situation to come to grips with for many people, and there is no shame in asking for help. Many organizations and sources of support are available if you seek them out. Again, if you read something here that makes you think you need help—ask for it; it is a sign of strength to ask for help, not a sign of weakness.

There are two major aspects to consider in this section: who we are and how IBM impacts us. Who we are is basically our personality. When we think of someone's personality, what are we talking about? Personality refers to the patterns of thinking, feeling, and behaving that characterize an individual. Each individual has a unique personality—no two people have identical personalities. When we compare two people, we will see differences between them based on their personality characteristics. Psychologists often use the idea of "traits" to describe these personality characteristics. Traits are often described as consistent and ongoing aspects of personality. They are relatively stable over time and situations, and they influence how we see life, our behavior, and our reactions.

Here are some examples.

- Extraversion (outgoing)—versus—introversion (shy).
- Agreeable—versus—hard to get along with.
- Dependable and reliable—versus—undependable and unreliable.
- Emotionally stable—versus—emotionally unstable.
- Open to new experiences—versus—close-minded.

The second aspect is how IBM will impact us as a disease, which will naturally vary widely depending on what IBM throws at us. This will impact factors like how IBM will affect our abilities and, in turn, the degree and type of life challenges we will face, the degree to which we will need to alter our life choices, and the level of fatigue we will have to deal with.

We have emphasized that the impact of IBM is quite variable. This also applies when we are talking about psychological impacts. Psychological impacts depend upon factors like the following.

- How old were you when symptoms emerged?
- How does it currently affect you physically?
- What impact does it currently have on your mobility?
- What impact does it currently have on your lifestyle?
- What impact does it have on your overall health?
- How fast is your progression?
- What supports do you have? Family, medical team, spiritual, psychological, other?
- How do you see your illness, your life now? Depressed, hopeless, realistic, optimistic, stoic?

Let us also take a moment to consider what is impacted by IBM. As we will see, just about every aspect of our everyday life is involved.

- How we now see ourselves and how we see our life (our thinking, attitudes, and our feelings)
- Independence (mobility / movement issues)
- Primary Relationships (parents / partner / children)
- Social Relations (friends / family / co-workers)
- Lifestyle (our day-to-day life routine)
- School and educational choices
- Finances: having a disability is expensive
- Career (job changes, long-term disability)
- Home and environment (house / car / etc.)
- Caregivers (Family members / agency [come into the home] / live in [employees who stay in your home])

6.4.1 Anxiety

Just what is anxiety? Anxiety is an emotion that is unpleasant and uncomfortable. It often makes us feel like something bad is about to happen. Anxiety has physical aspects similar to stress. We feel restless and tense and on edge. Anxiety is often a normal reaction to a situation that causes stress. For example, I have anxiety before I go for a job interview. Anxiety tends to be stronger than everyday worry and lasts longer. There are different types of anxiety, and there are different ways anxiety can cause trouble for us, as we will explore here.

It is normal for people to have "future anxiety." We wonder and worry about what may happen tomorrow. Many people have anxiety over the future, especially if some event is coming up. The day before a game, the hockey player will have anxiety about how they're going to play. Having a dynamic disease like IBM intensifies this anxiety over the future. Where will my weakness strike next? Will I fall tomorrow? What will happen if . . .?

It's not unusual for people to struggle with day-to-day "general" anxiety; nowadays, it seems like a regular part of our hectic lives. Specific problems intensify daily anxiety levels, and having IBM is certainly a good reason to have anxiety.

It is essential to understand that fear and anxiety help us avoid danger. Imagine walking in a forest and seeing a snake. You immediately become fearful, feel anxious and jump back. For a few moments, you are full of adrenaline and energy. This is an adaptive response designed to save your life (and this response is not a problem if it saves your life).

On the other hand, anxiety can become a crippling problem if you imagine a snake that isn't there. You have all this stress and anxiety produced just from thinking about the snake. Here, IBM may become the imaginary snake we can't stop thinking about. Having anxiety over long periods is not healthy, either psychologically or physically.

> *During the early phase of my disease, my mother was in the hospital, dying of cancer. Every night I returned from the hospital, my muscles had knots like golf balls from the stress. At that time, I was not diagnosed, and my anxiety over my undiagnosed illness and my mother was too much for me. It came out in muscle tension.*

It's a struggle to deal with the stresses of life, and it's a constant problem that we need to work on. In Chapter 7, I will provide the titles of some helpful books on anxiety.

- Often, people imagine what might happen tomorrow and develop intense anxiety over it.
- People with IBM may fixate on "future anxiety."
- Many try to deal with this anxiety using denial.
- Controlling "future anxiety" is the most challenging point

discussed here, and it is critically important:

- Knowledge can help ground a runaway imagination.
- We need to focus on today and live for today.
- We need to learn to relax, let the future unfold, and "take life one day at a time."

6.4.2 Stress management

Like anxiety, stress is a normal reaction designed to help us respond to new situations and avoid danger. Stress is triggered in the brain when we perceive or think about something that implies danger. The brain tells the body to get ready to fight, freeze or run away. These changes in the body involve a series of chemical releases that significantly impact the body's organs.

Again, like anxiety, stress can be triggered by perceiving something in the real world, like the snake on the pathway, and also by simply imagining the snake. A good example might be: I leave the house, and I get to the store. I suddenly think, "Did I leave the stove on?" This idea triggers my stress reaction. The more I think about this, and the more I wonder—did I leave it on?—the more stress I experience.

I feel stressed, but I'm often not aware of the physical impacts—I'm not aware of the chemicals surging through my body. Sometimes the physical stress reaction becomes obvious. For example, as you drive over the hill at eighty miles an hour and see a police car—that sudden uncomfortable feeling in your stomach is the release of those stress chemicals!

There are two cases where stress really becomes a problem: frequent, exceptionally high stress for short periods—or elevated stress over long periods. Stress chemicals dramatically impact the systems and organs of the body, putting them under tremendous strain. Over time, this adds wear and tear to our bodies. The physical effects of stress can impact the heart, the immune system, the digestive system, the muscular system, and the skin. High or chronic stress is associated with many health risks, including heart attack and stroke, high blood pressure, diabetes, acid reflux, and tension headaches.

Stress influences our emotions and feelings, often making us feel on edge, depressed, moody, and overwhelmed. Stress makes us worry, have problems concentrating, and can impact our judgment. Over time, stress can make us feel helpless and out of control.

You cannot be both stressed and relaxed at the same time. They are opposites, like the two ends of a teeter-totter. If stress goes up, relaxation goes down. If relaxation goes up, stress goes down. This way of understanding stress points to an important internal mechanism we can all use to deal with stress.

When you feel stressed, you can learn to relax mentally. For example, many people develop a calm scene that they associate with feeling relaxed. Imagine the last time you were at your favorite beach, watching the sunset while listening to the water. You'd never felt so relaxed in your life. With practice, you can reinforce this feeling of relaxation every time you imagine the beach. When you feel stressed and visualize the beach, your relaxation response kicks in and brings down your stress. There are many different relaxation techniques and strategies that you can learn.

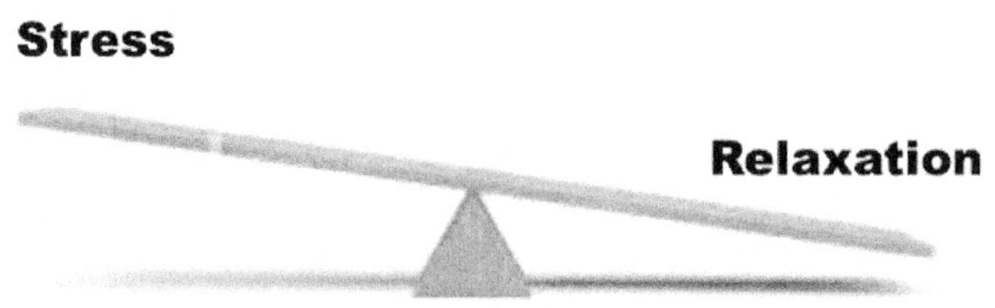

Figure 16 The stress relaxation teeter-totter.

Ideally, you can also learn to prevent a lot of stress. Generally, the better your overall health, the better you can handle stress. This includes diet, drinking enough (non-alcoholic beverages), getting good exercise, regularly relaxing, identifying those things that cause you to have stress, and dealing with them or learning how to avoid them.

Finally, many people deal with stress inappropriately. Many people drink alcohol to relieve feelings of stress, or they smoke. Unfortunately, drinking and smoking add to the physical problems caused by stress.

Stress (whatever causes it) creates a series of mental and physical impacts on people.

- Stress is normal, but two types are harmful.
    - Short periods of extreme stress (acute stress).
    - Moderately raised stress for a long time (chronic).
- People with IBM must be aware of stress and learn to manage it.
- Working with a therapist may be very helpful.
- Mental aspects are part of the solution (how we see our stress, learn to cope/relax, and our attitude).
- A healthy physical lifestyle is part of the solution (Smoking? Drinking? Diet? Proper exercise?).

6.4.3 Emotions

This section will discuss emotions and explore some of the common feelings of patients with IBM. First, I will talk about the difference between emotions and feelings. Emotions are physical states that we experience in the body. They are produced by the brain and involve a series of chemical impacts (just as stress does, but with different chemicals). Emotions are physical and involve physical changes in the body.

Feelings, on the other hand, are what we subjectively interpret emotions as. We experience an emotion, then assign a name and a meaning to it. Let me give a couple of examples. Your partner has been away for a few days on a business trip. When you meet them at the airport, your eyes light up, and you are overwhelmed by emotion; maybe you start to cry. You realize how much you have missed them. We interpret this emotion as feelings of love. Or you have been waiting in line for half an hour. It is finally your turn, and someone steps in front of you and says, "I need to go ahead. I'm in a hurry." Your face turns red, and your teeth clench. That emotion is anger, and our feeling is irritation, aggravation, and frustration.

It is not uncommon for people to be poor at naming or describing their emotions and feelings. Generally speaking, it's helpful to be aware of our feelings and ask ourselves if the situation justifies our feelings. Often, if people think about it, they may realize that their feeling does not correspond to the situation or that the strength of their feeling does not match the problem—perhaps the feeling is either too great or too little.

Being aware of our feelings also gives us another advantage. When we have an uncomfortable feeling and are aware of it, we can do something about it. We don't have to be passive victims of our feelings. For example, let's say my coworker made an offhand comment at lunch about the accessibility of the building. Later as I sat there and thought about it, I got irritated because my coworker did not understand how important access is for some of our clients. I decided to talk to him during the coffee break, and I explained how I felt. He seemed to understand what I was talking about, and I felt much better. I took action to resolve my irritation.

Emotions and feelings also significantly impact thinking, and thinking substantially affects how we feel. As well we often mix up thoughts and feelings. Someone may say, "I feel like I'm not good enough." That is not a feeling; that is a thought. Thoughts are ideas and opinions. When thoughts last a long time, we talk about them as our attitudes towards things.

Thinking about something can result in a feeling—I'm thinking about the test tomorrow, which is making me feel anxious. Feelings influence thinking. If you are anxious about the test, you won't think or remember well.

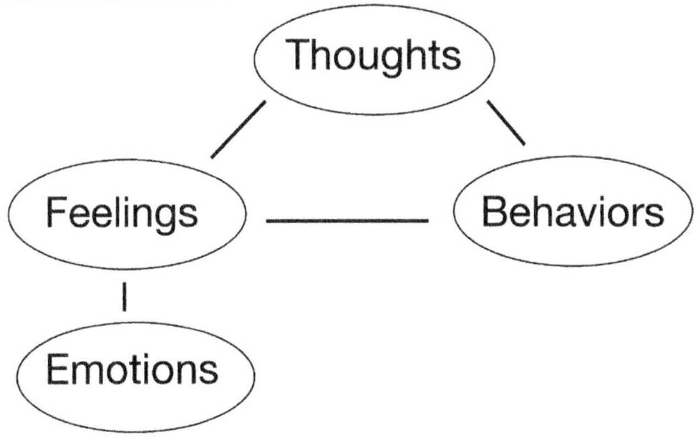

Figure 17 The relationships of feeling, thoughts, and behaviors.

People tend to have more positive thoughts about the world when they feel happy. Feelings and thoughts also influence behavior and often motivate our behavior. We act because we think and we feel. It also goes the other way—when we act, it affects how we think and feel. For example, if I am at bat and swing and hit a home run, I will think I'm a good baseball player and feel happy. If I strike out, I may think the umpire was a poor judge of the pitcher's throws, and I'll think I was robbed and feel bad.

It is a healthy and positive exercise for you to take a moment and write down how you feel about having IBM and what your thoughts are about having IBM. Think about it for a moment—how do your thoughts and feelings about IBM influence your behavior? How do they influence your attitudes? How do your attitudes affect how you see, think about, and feel about having IBM? Don't be afraid to discuss how you think and feel about IBM with your family and caregivers.

One of the questions that often comes up is: "Is this feeling normal?" There is no right or wrong way to feel. How you feel is how you feel and represents a normal response. Everyone will feel differently about things because we are different people with different experiences in life, and we all see life somewhat differently. So, it's only natural that our feelings will also differ.

Often people with IBM describe a roller coaster of feelings going from very positive to very negative. It's essential to be open to both positive and negative feelings because they equally describe your situation at the time. However, if you can, it is generally healthier to focus on the good feelings, appreciate the positive, and at the same time, try to get through and rise above the hard times.

- "Is it normal to feel this way?"
- No matter how you feel, it is a normal reaction for you.
- There are no "right" or "wrong" feelings.
- Roller coaster: We will all have many positive and negative feelings.
- It is essential to be open to both our happy and sad feelings and not deny them.
- To experience all of our feelings is a natural and essential part of our lives and learning.
- It is important to get through and rise above bad times.
- Have gratitude and appreciate the good times.
- Focus on the positive more than the negative.

6.4.4. Depression

At first, it is common to feel sad over the effects of IBM. It is also a natural feeling to be sad when we can no longer participate in the everyday activities of life. What is the relationship between sadness and depression?

Sadness is a normal feeling in response to something that makes us unhappy. It is a typical response to experiencing a minor loss. Sadness is considered a mood and is a brief feeling that may last minutes, hours, or perhaps a day.

Likewise, it is normal to feel bouts of mild depression where we feel a more significant loss. Mild depression is characterized by feelings of sadness, low energy, problems sleeping, problems concentrating, feeling you need to be alone, or changes in eating habits. Mild episodes of depression (and anxiety) are common in facing the diagnosis and experience of IBM. These are expected and normal feelings in the face of a major life challenge. Try to allow yourself to experience and work through these feelings.

Take bad days one at a time. Try not to dwell on the negative. When you feel depressed, try to think of positive actions to make yourself feel better. Appreciate positive things. Spend time doing things that make you happy, even if you feel down. You may not want to get out of bed, but it's essential that you do. Try to maintain your regular daily routine until you feel better.

In summary, short periods of sadness and even more extended periods of mild depression are normal and expected when facing a significant challenge like IBM. Try to look to the positive and work through the negative.

Major depression is a different story; it is a medical problem that needs treatment. What is major depression? Four criteria point to major depression: length, intensity, impact, and thoughts of suicide. It is a concern if you have depression that lasts more than two weeks. The intensity of your feelings includes profound feelings of depression with little hope of returning to normal. Major depression disrupts the normal, routine activities of life. People commonly lose their appetite, feel exhausted, lose motivation, cannot concentrate or focus on tasks, see no solutions, and stop communicating with the people in their lives. Common feelings include a sense of hopelessness and the feeling that there will never be a solution—that things will never get better. Finally, thoughts of suicide often occur during deep depression. They do not simply occur "out of the blue."

Any of these indicators of major depression should lead you to your doctor. Major depression does not merely "go away." A combination of medication and counseling helps in most cases.

Unfortunately, there is often a feeling of anxiety associated with dealing with depression, and many people do not seek help because they feel ashamed. If you feel depressed, please approach your family and your doctor. Although it may feel hopeless, you have to remember that, at this time, you are not seeing life clearly, and you need help to get back on track.

A factor complicating emotionally dealing with IBM is the presence and severity of complications. For example, difficulty swallowing has social impacts when the patient becomes embarrassed or afraid to eat in public or with friends. This can lead to isolation and feelings of depression. Likewise, changes in speech may cause a patient to curtail social activities. Again, I emphasize the importance of identifying complications early and working with your doctor and others to deal with these issues both physically and psychologically.

Sadness versus depression.

- Sadness is a normal emotion in response to something that makes you feel unhappy.
- Sadness is a fleeting feeling; it lasts a few hours or a day. It's normal: we all feel sad at times.
- Depression is a more prolonged, profound feeling of being empty, down, flat, etc.

- It lasts at least a few weeks; involves broad, adverse changes in outlook.
- It may develop into a significant problem.

Minor depression: A major factor.

- Mild, brief bouts of anxiety and depression are common and expected when faced with IBM.
- Let yourself "Live/work through" these feelings: it's O.K. to feel down sometimes.
- Take things one small step at a time.
- Try not to focus on the negative aspects.
- Appreciate and focus on gratitude for the positive.
- Try to turn negative feelings into positives: if you feel sad, what is a positive action you can take to deal with it?
- A positive attitude is your best asset.
- Spend more time doing things that make you happy.

Major depression: A medical problem.

- The red flags of major depression:
  - Length: lasting for more than two weeks.
  - Intensity: deep negative feelings, loss of hope.
  - Impact: normal, routine life activities are disrupted:
    - Loss of appetite, feeling exhausted, loss of motivation, lack of focus, hopelessness, and no future/no solutions.
    - Thoughts of self-harm or suicide.
- Mention depression to your medical team.
- Counseling is a good idea for those with IBM and is often effective in dealing with depression.
- Many are helped by taking medication.
- Do not suffer in silence: talk to someone.

6.4.5 Psychological stages.

The idea of psychological stages is widespread, and many people have heard about stages of development (e.g., infancy, early childhood, preschool, school age, adolescence, young adulthood, middle adulthood, maturity) and grief (e.g., denial, anger, bargaining, depression, acceptance). In my opinion, because people are so different, there is no one set of stages people go through when confronting a diagnosis of IBM. I believe there are two reasons for this. First, we are all so different in how we deal with these things, and these differences can be influenced by multiple factors in our lives, such as our upbringing. Second, we are not all physically impacted by IBM in the same way.

One problem is that if you read about stages, you may feel something is wrong with you if you don't follow the "proper sequence." In my opinion, the main value of the idea of stages in terms of IBM is to understand that you will likely experience a shifting range of perspectives and feelings as you deal with IBM. This is a natural response to the new and different challenges IBM presents in your life as time goes on. Someone asked me if I was angry about having IBM. I replied, "No, why would I be angry"? The lady said, "Oh, you haven't reached the angry stage yet." I will never reach the "angry stage" because I don't see the rationale or the point of getting angry at something I cannot control.

6.4.6 Denial

Sigmund Freud, a famous psychologist, believed that people develop psychological "defense mechanisms." These are unconscious methods we use to avoid the stress and anxiety of life. In many cases, defense mechanisms successfully allow us to avoid problems and anxiety. However, defense mechanisms intended to help us can also end up causing us problems in the long term.

When we are first challenged with the diagnosis of IBM, shock and disbelief are probably two of the first reactions we have. It takes some time to come to grips with and mentally process the idea. Most people do eventually succeed in accepting and acknowledging their situation. On the other hand, the other day, a person said to me: "I have had IBM for some twenty years and have no interest in knowing about IBM or how far it has progressed." This person's statement appears to reflect the defense mechanism of denial. In a nutshell, denial is refusing to admit the truth about something.

Many people try to deny the situation altogether. If you don't think about it and don't acknowledge it, then it is "out of sight, out of mind." Unfortunately, IBM is not the sort of thing that you can ignore—it will not merely go away.

Denial is a dangerous problem in IBM because turning a blind eye to your health often delays identifying and managing complications. As we have seen above, there can be serious complications involved in IBM, and if left untreated, they can lead to serious consequences.

Figure 18 Denial.

If you see someone in denial, it may be beneficial to talk to them and see how they feel: what is their perspective on the situation? Do they see any consequences in not dealing with the situation? Why are they afraid to face the problem? Do their thoughts about the problem make sense? Or are they looking at the situation "through the wrong end of the telescope?" Can you help the person find some middle ground where they feel comfortable and begin acknowledging the situation? Often support from a good friend or loved one can help.

Dealing with denial takes time, many small steps and minor victories before the curtain can be pulled open. Do not be judgmental, and give lots of time and support to individuals in denial (including yourself) to help them see that they can and should deal with the situation.

6.4.7 Blame

When something goes wrong, it is often human nature to look for someone or something to blame. People often feel uncomfortable when they don't know why something happens. Assigning blame "points the finger" for your problems to a specific cause. "It was the medications I took that caused my IBM." "The new carpet we put in the house gave off a chemical." "It was the stress of my new job." When we feel like we know what caused our problems, it makes us feel better. To think that IBM just struck us out of the blue, for no understandable reason, with no way to prevent it, is a frightening idea because it makes us feel helpless and vulnerable.

As well, it's common for people to blame themselves. This usually leads to a spiral of feeling guilt. "If I got this illness, I must have done something to deserve it." If you could look at this objectively, you would see that this thinking is faulty; is it your fault that lightning hit your house?

- Blame is a common reaction when you feel bad or something bad happens to you.
- Blaming IBM on "X" may make you feel better.
- People often blame themselves, causing guilt.
- It is hard to accept, but IBM's triggers are likely beyond anyone's control or prevention.
- Blaming something or someone for one's illness is ultimately a waste of valuable energy, often leading to frustration and bitterness.

6.4.8 Acceptance

As I said above, it is usually uncomfortable for people when something major happens in their lives, and they don't have an explanation for *why* it happened. Although challenging, this is something you must face: you must accept that you have this illness, whatever caused it, and move forward with your life.

Accepting IBM is very difficult for another reason. Because you also have to face the slow decline in your abilities that comes with IBM, acceptance and adaptation must occur hand-in-hand as you slowly learn to live "life with IBM." As new challenges come along, we constantly make small adjustments and adapt to new situations—new realities. For example, the new reality may be that we can no longer drive. Or that we need help in the bathroom. These are significant challenges because they impact the fundamental ways in which we see ourselves. Our focus needs to be on ongoing adaptations and acceptance in small steps. IBM challenges us to be stronger, smarter, and more organized, but it also challenges us to be more forgiving of ourselves, to accept what we cannot change, and to make the best of life as we encounter it.

Many people are looking for an identity. For example, many people define themselves by their jobs. I am a lawyer; I am a doctor; I am a bus driver. Many define themselves based on their role in life. I am a father; I am a mother; I am a son. I have met some people obsessed with defining themselves based on their illnesses. Do not lose yourself in your diagnosis of IBM. You are still you—you with IBM, but still you. Accept IBM in your life, but do not become it.

- No one wants to be ill; it is not something we would choose.
- However, we were not given a choice—this is how it is: "It is what it is."
- I am still me; I have IBM—don't let IBM define you.
- How we "see" this and deal with it makes a big difference to the kind of life we will live.
- Accept that life will change and be different and adapt to get the most out of life as it unfolds.
- Acceptance and adaptation are complex and take time—they may occur in small steps for the rest of your life.
- Coping with IBM challenges us to face and rise above many everyday problems.

6.4.9 Perspective

Perspective means how we see life. Each of us has a slightly different perspective because we see life from slightly different points of view. Ideally, our perspective will be accurate enough to reflect reality the way it really is in life. So, if two people stand beside each other and look at something, they should describe essentially the same view.

IBM is a disease that sometimes robs people of accurate perspective. We don't look at it as it is. For example, look at the picture below.

Figure 19 The loss of perspective.

If our perception is clear, we will immediately see a fork and probably think nothing of it. Likewise, if we see IBM accurately, then we can deal with it realistically. On the other hand, when people are under stress, they may not see things accurately; in this case, they may focus on the shadow and not the fork. If we don't see IBM with a clear perspective and we see it based on our fears or based on the unknown, then we may end up confused and even frightened—IBM may become like the shadow in the picture. We may lose sight of what we know about IBM and how to adapt, and our fears may take over.

Sometimes our feelings influence our perspective; this is common when dealing with IBM. Depression and exhaustion may color our view and may lead us to have a distorted perception of IBM.

We need to keep IBM in perspective. As we have seen above, IBM does impact longevity, but not to the same degree that other conditions can. If you are diagnosed at age 55, you will likely live another 30 years. Let's contrast IBM with ALS. On average, people with ALS will die within five years of diagnosis.

It is not helpful to see IBM in an overly negative light. Talk to other patients with IBM, talk to your doctor, and talk to your family to check your perspective. If you see IBM as a mountain too high to climb, it has already defeated you. On the other hand, if you see the individual steps on the path, you can take them one at a time and not be overwhelmed.

6.4.10 Suicide

I have spoken with patients who have expressed that "suicide is the only alternative after an IBM diagnosis." If we see IBM accurately and judge it fairly, it is not a monster that we need to feel hopeless in the face of.

I have done my best to draw an accurate picture of IBM. Not optimistic, not pessimistic, but hopefully a realistic picture. The good: most people should live out an essentially average life span after the diagnosis of IBM. IBM does not impair thinking or memory. IBM progresses slowly, giving you time to adapt psychologically and time to adapt your physical environment. In the early stages, a well-designed, individualized exercise program should help. We understand the common complications in IBM, and generally, they can be managed.

The bad: IBM eventually severely affects movement in the hands, arms, and legs, making daily activities difficult or impossible. There is currently no effective medical treatment for IBM. Complications can become life-threatening, especially if ignored or not managed properly.

Some people may only see the shadow and not the fork. Life after diagnosis may seem hopeless, and their perspective on what is possible and what awaits them may become distorted to the point of despair. Suicide may seem like a solution when this happens. This is especially true if you have endured long periods of fatigue and depression or struggled with significant problems swallowing. If you think that suicide may be a solution, it is helpful to double-check your perspective with someone else.

As we described above, thoughts of suicide are often a result of major depression. Unfortunately, we are often afraid to ask for help if we have suicidal thoughts. We are worried that we will be seen as weak or that the other person may brush us off and think nothing is wrong. It takes courage to reach out, but today there are many treatment options for depression, and you should give yourself the chance to explore these options. Talk to your doctor.

While suicide may seem like a solution to you, keep in mind that it has a tremendous impact on families and those left behind; furthermore, quite sadly, some people attempt suicide and end up in a worse situation than they started with.

In summary, we need to keep IBM in perspective. It is not helpful to see IBM in an overly positive or negative light. Talk to people and check your perspective. It's okay to talk with friends and family, but I suggest that you don't rely on them exclusively; they may feel overwhelmed themselves and not know how best to support you.

If you feel depressed and have suicidal thoughts, medications and counseling may help, and I urge you to reach out and talk to someone. Talk to your doctor or counselor. Talk about depression. However challenging life is right this minute, you are still here and still alive. Try to appreciate that. Recognize that when you are depressed, you may not be able to see the positive possibilities that exist all around you and ahead of you.

- IBM often has drastic impacts on one's life.
- For some, suicide may seem like a solution.
- Suicide usually has a significant impact on families.
- A suicide attempt may fail and one may end up worse off.
- Are your feelings from deep depression or a realistic appraisal of your physical situation and illnesses?

- If your feelings are from depression, treatments may help you.
- If you have reached the point where you cannot go on, then reaching out to others for help would seem like the best step.

6.4.11 End-of-life

Our views about death have changed dramatically over the last fifty years. No one mentioned people dying when I was a child in the late 50s and early 60s. Death was cloaked in mystery, even in medicine. How medicine dealt with the end of life has also changed dramatically. Today we are much more open about talking about death.

In 2016, I ended up in intensive care with a pulmonary embolism. One of the first things they did was ask me to tell them what resuscitation level I wanted—essentially, high, medium, or none. I was slightly surprised by this question, and I joked to the nurse, "I'm not that sick, am I?" She said, "It's better for everyone if we know your wishes, and we ask everyone."

Today, medicine has a new and more open approach to understanding end-of-life. It is now common for people to discuss end-of-life planning with their families and doctors. This is especially important in older individuals with multiple medical conditions (it is common to have more than one health problem as we get older). Having various issues complicates the management of each one. If you have IBM in conjunction with other health issues, or if you have IBM and have severe complications, it might be helpful for you to discuss end-of-life options with your family and doctor. Today, the emphasis is on having a pain, and stress-free passing. Pre-planning gives you and your doctor control over the situation.

- With proper medical management, most patients with IBM

will die with IBM, not from IBM.

- IBM is not considered a fatal disease.
- Complications are usually not fatal if well managed.
- IBM is a disease of aging; as we age, various other health issues may lead to death.
- IBM complicates one's other medical issues.
- Our medical team must manage our illnesses.
- It is wrong to see IBM as a death sentence.

End-of-life options and choices.

- Depending upon where you live, there may be options your medical team may be able to offer you to make your passing easier.
- In some cases of IBM, especially those involving severe complications, it may be helpful to explore end-of-life options. There are better choices available than suicide.
- As you age and problems arise, discussing the various end-of-life options with your family and your medical team is essential.
- Like the security of having a will, this planning may help reduce the stress and anxiety of your passing.

6.4.12 Compassion

An essential part of coping with IBM is having compassion for yourself, your family, and others.

Have compassion and understanding for yourself. Understand when you can't do what you want to do. You're not lazy, and if you could, you would. Try to have compassion for others who have different struggles, stressors, and anxieties, because ultimately, they fight the same fight you do.

Encourage others to be compassionate and show understanding. Often, people are harsh and cruel because they do not understand. Our job is to understand this illness we call IBM and to help educate others. Education overcomes ignorance. Be a firm but compassionate advocate for yourself and others.

- Have understanding for yourself.
- Have compassion for others in your life and their stress, anxiety, and problems.
- Encourage others to be compassionate.
- Many people simply are uninformed about illnesses.
- Education overcomes ignorance.
- Become a "calm but strong" advocate for yourself and others, not just for the ill but for everyone you meet.

6.5 COUNSELING

You are not alone and cannot be expected to deal with IBM single-handedly. But this is not just about doctors and tests. It's also the realization that you might benefit from talking with a mental health professional. You deserve help if needed, and help is available if you ask. There is no shame in seeking advice and support, and today many avenues to access resources easily are available. Many counselors and coaches offer video services that are easy to take advantage of.

As I've already said, as IBM challenges your mobility, it can also threaten your sense of who you are, because as your mobility becomes limited and your routines change, your sense of yourself also changes. Having someone professional to talk with can be a lifesaver if you open yourself to the possibility. This applies to you and those close to you, as they also have to learn to adapt and face the same life-altering challenges that you do. Do not let pride get in the way of helping yourself.

6.6 FAITH

Many find meaning and comfort in faith, and their belief gives them strength in facing challenges. Faith may be observed by participating in a large organized religion or in more private ways. However you experience and express it, faith is an integral part of your life. Use its gift and power to help confront the frustrations introduced by IBM. There is nothing incompatible with combining faith with the latest advances in medicine.

6.7 BEST PRACTICES AND TIPS

- If you are in the diagnostic process, be strong and advocate for yourself until you have an answer.
- Find a good doctor you are comfortable with and see them regularly.
- See yourself as a professional patient: see being a patient as your job.
- Learn about IBM. Read different websites for information.
- Follow your symptoms looking for changes and complications; communicate clearly with your doctor and listen to their advice.
- Respect and communicate clearly with those who are looking after you.
- Recognize the stress and extra work IBM puts on your loved ones, and be kind and compassionate with them. Don't let them overdo it.
- Be kind and compassionate to yourself and others.
- Monitor your stress and mental health: if you feel depressed, seek out help.
- Join a Facebook group and meet other patients with IBM. Those ahead of you on the path can help you with your journey.

- Stick up for yourself and other mobility-challenged patients.
- Take care of yourself and your family: seek counseling.
- I have found that the best way to help myself is to help others.

6.8 PSYCHOLOGICAL ASPECTS: KEY POINTS

- Coping with a chronic illness is a major psychological challenge.
- Anxiety and depression are common.
- Severe depression or thoughts of suicide should be addressed with your doctor.
- Weakness challenges us to be better organized, deal with our stress effectively and make good life choices.
- Acceptance is better than blame, denial, or bitterness.
- Keep IBM in proper perspective.
- Look at yourself with compassion
- Seek help and help others.
- Discussions about end-of-life planning are suggested.

Chapter 7: Summary and Further Resources

7.1 SUMMARY

We have a life-altering disease that has no cure. It is rare, affects people differently, and can significantly impact one's ability to live a normal life. Weakness in the arms and legs compromises our mobility. Having a dynamic disorder where the goalposts of our abilities keep moving is very challenging and calls for ongoing adaptations.

We do not control getting this illness or its physical impacts, but we control how we see it and our attitude toward it. IBM will change how you see yourself. If we let it, it can become an insurmountable mountain that disheartens and defeats us. On the other hand, we can choose to see it as the challenge that it is and meet this challenge with innovative and flexible ways to adapt.

I believe that knowledge is our friend in confronting this illness. The more we know, the better we can deal with what this disease throws at us. The more we know, the better we can cope and adapt. If we take a positive approach to deal with changes and seize opportunities, we can be happy and live meaningful lives.

7.2 FURTHER RESOURCES

7.2.1 Books

Many books are available to help people deal with the issues we have discussed. I have suggested a few here. I find it helpful to use a service like Amazon because the ratings given by other readers can help you choose a good book.

Bernhard, T. (2015). *How to live well with chronic pain and illness: A mindful guide.* Simon & Schuster.

Bourne, E. J. (2015). *The anxiety and phobia workbook.* New Harbinger.

Bowler, K. (2018). *Everything happens for a reason: And other lies I've loved.* Random House.

Brewer, J. (2021). *Unwinding anxiety: New science shows how to break the cycles of worry and fear to heal your mind.* Penguin.

Carbonell, D. A. (2016). *The worry trick: How worry controls you and what you can do to take back your life*. New Harbinger.

Cohen, L. M. (2019). *A dignified ending: Taking control over how we die*. Rowman & Littlefield Publishers.

Craske, M. G., & Barlow, D. H. (2007). Mastery of your anxiety and panic: Workbook for primary care settings. Oxford University Press.

Davis, M. (2009). *The relaxation and stress reduction workbook.* New Harbinger.

Jacqueline, I. (2018). *Surviving and thriving with an invisible chronic illness: How to stay sane, calm the chaos, and live one step ahead of your most inconvenient symptoms.* Raincoast Books.

Kalanithi, P. (2016). *When breath becomes air.* Random House.

Knaus, W. J. (2008). *The cognitive behavioral workbook for anxiety: A step-by-step program.* New Harbinger.

Kross, E. (2021). *Chatter: The voice in our head, why it matters, and how to harness it*. Crown.

LeFort, S. M., Webster, L., Lorig, K., Holman, H., Sobel, D., Laurent,

D., & Gonzalez, V. (2015). *Living a healthy life with chronic pain* (4th ed.). Bull Publishing

Levitin, D. J. (2015). *The organized mind: Thinking straight in the age of information overload.* Penguin.

Livheim, F., Bond, F. W., Hedensjo, B. S., & Ek, D. (2018). *The mindfulness and acceptance workbook for stress reduction: Using acceptance and commitment therapy to manage stress, build resilience, and create the life you want.* New Harbinger.

Lorig, K. (2018). *Building better caregivers. A caregiver's guide to reducing stress and staying healthy.* Bull Publishing.

Miller, T. (2021). *What doesn't kill you: A life with chronic illness - Lessons from a body in revolt.* Henry Holt and Company.

Morin, A. (2014). *13 things mentally strong people don't do: Take back your power, embrace change, face your fears, and train your brain for happiness and success.* William Morrow.

Shannon, J. (2017). *Don't feed the monkey mind: How to stop the cycle of anxiety, fear, and worry.* New Harbinger.

Weber, J. (2019). *Be calm: Proven techniques to stop anxiety now.* Althea Press.

7.2.2 Links

Here are several credible links you can click on:

Information about IBM

Johns Hopkins Myositis Centre – IBM overview

https://www.youtube.com/watch?v=Fo1yhVPHmws

Johns Hopkins Myositis Centre – Signs and symptoms

https://www.youtube.com/watch?v=YU0TrMRS1GU

Johns Hopkins Myositis Centre – Diagnosis

https://www.youtube.com/watch?v=2B8P-9LtYq4

Johns Hopkins myositis Center – Treatment

https://www.youtube.com/watch?v=8MfnpobNurY

Johns Hopkins Myositis Centre – Lifestyle options

https://www.youtube.com/watch?v=5zfASzBQ1zM

Muscular Dystrophy Association: IBM

https://www.mda.org/disease/inclusion-body-myositis

The Myositis Association: Brochure on IBM (PDF)

http://www.ibmmyositis.com/IBMbrochure.pdf

The Myositis Association: Can stem cells cure myositis?

https://www.myositis.org/about-myositis/treatment-disease-management/can-stem-cells-cure-myositis/

Myositis Support & Understanding: IBM

https://understandingmyositis.org/myositis/inclusion-body-myositis/

Cure IBM

https://cureibm.org

Inclusion Body Myositis (by William Tillier)

http://www.ibmmyositis.com/index.htm

Exercise and IBM

Exercise and Physical Therapy

https://www.myositis.org/about-myositis/treatment-disease-management/exercise-physical-therapy/

Exercise in Place

https://understandingmyositis.org/exercise-and-myositis/

Research and Clinical Trials

Developing an IBM stem cell approach

http://aavogen.com

Clinical Trials USA

https://clinicaltrials.gov/

IBM Disease Registry at Yale

https://ysph.yale.edu/ibmregistry/about/%22/

Patient organizations and support

The Myositis Association

https://www.myositis.org/patient-support/support-groups/

Myositis Canada

https://www.myositis.ca

Myositis Association Australia

https://myositis.org.au

Myositis UK

https://www.myositis.org.uk

Myositis Support & Understanding Private IBM Support Group

https://www.facebook.com/groups/inclusionbodymyositis/

Other

Muscular Dystrophy UK: IBM Alert Card

https://www.musculardystrophyuk.org/static/s3fs-public/2020-03/Alert-Card-IBM.pdf

Peter Frampton

https://www.brainandlife.org/articles/peter-frampton-found-new-purpose-after-inclusion-body-myositis-diagnosis

7.2.3 References

Anand, U., Pacchetti, B., Anand, P., & Sodergren, M. H. (2021). Cannabis-based medicines and pain: A review of potential synergistic and entourage effects. *Pain Management, 11*(4), 395-403. https://doi.org/10.2217/pmt-2020-0110

Badrising, U. A., Maat-Schieman, M. L. C., Houwelingen, J. C., Doorn, P. A., Duinen, S. G., Engelen, B. G. M., Faber, C. G., Hoogendijk, J. E., Jager, A. E., Koehler, P. J., Visser, M., Verschuuren, J. J. G. M., & Wintzen, A. R. (2005). Inclusion body myositis: Clinical features and clinical course of the disease in 64 patients. *Journal of Neurology, 252*(12), 1448-1454. https://doi.org/10.1007/s00415-005-0884-y

Bhashyam, A., Lubinus, M., Filmore, E., Wilson, L., Williams, J., Gonzalez Ramos, O., & Bhai, S. (2022). Pain profile and opioid medication use in patients with idiopathic inflammatory myopathies. *Rheumatology*, keac271. https://doi.org/10.1093/rheumatology/keac271

Bjornevik, K., Cortese, M., Healy, B. C., Kuhle, J., Mina, M. J., Leng, Y., Elledge, S. J., Niebuhr, D. W., Scher, A. I., Munger, K. L., & Ascherio, A. (2022). Longitudinal analysis reveals high prevalence of Epstein-Barr virus associated with multiple sclerosis. *Science, 375*(6578), 296-301. https://doi.org/10.1126/science.abj8222

Boyaji, S., Merkow, J., Elman, R. N. M., Kaye, A. D., Yong, R. J., & Urman, R. D. (2020). The role of Cannabidiol (CBD) in chronic pain management: An assessment of current evidence. *Current Pain and Headache Reports, 24*(2). https://doi.org/10.1007/s11916-020-0835-4

Brokamp, G., Hurst, L., Hartog, L., Vilson, F., Reynolds, J., Elsheikh, B. H., & Arnold, W. D. (2022). Characterizing ventilatory muscle dysfunction in inclusion body myositis. American Journal of Physical Medicine & Rehabilitation, Publish Ahead of Print. https://doi.org/10.1097/PHM.0000000000002114

Caneiro, J. P., Bunzli, S., & O'Sullivan, P. (2021). Beliefs about the body and pain: The critical role in musculoskeletal pain management. *Brazilian Journal of Physical Therapy*, *25*(1), 17-29. https://doi.org/10.1016/j.bjpt.2020.06.003

Cohen, S. P., Vase, L., & Hooten, W. M. (2021). Chronic pain: An update on burden, best practices, and new advances. *The Lancet*, *397*(10289), 2082-2097. https://doi.org/10.1016/S0140-6736(21)00393-7

Dardis, C., Antezana, A., Tanji, K., & Maccabee, P. J. (2017). Inclusion body myositis: A case presenting with respiratory failure and autopsy findings leading to the hypothesis of a paraneoplastic cause. *American Journal of Case Reports, 18*, 700-706. https://doi.org/10.12659/AJCR.903566

Doleys, D. M. (2014). *Pain: Dynamics and complexities*. Oxford University Press.

FDA, 2019. https://www.fda.gov/consumers/consumer-updates/fda-warns-about-stem-cell-therapies

Gorina Y, Hoyert D, Lentzner H, Goulding M. (2006). Trends in causes of death among older persons in the United States. *Aging Trends*, No 6. Hyattsville, Maryland: National Center for Health Statistics.

Goyal, N. A., & Mozaffar, T. (2021). Dysphagia in inclusion body myositis, A Disease of the Elderly. *OBM Geriatrics, 5*(1). https://doi.org/10.21926/obm.geriatr.2101154

Greenberg, S. A. (2016). Inclusion Body Myositis. *CONTINUUM: Lifelong Learning in Neurology, 22*(21), 1871-1888. https://doi.org/10.1212/01.CON.0000511071.58338.1e

Greenberg, S. A. (2019). Inclusion body myositis: Clinical features and pathogenesis. *Nature Reviews Rheumatology*, *15*, 257-272. https://doi.org/10.1038/s41584-019-0186-x

Greenberg, S. A. (2021). Counting People with Inclusion Body Myositis. *Neurology,* 10.1212/WNL.0000000000011994. https://doi.org/10.1212/WNL.0000000000011994

Jørgensen, A., Jensen, K., Nielsen, J., Frandsen, U., Hvid, L., Bjørnshauge, M., Diederichsen, L., & Aagaard, P. (2022). Effects of blood-flow restricted resistance training on mechanical muscle function and thigh lean mass in sIBM patients. *Scandinavian Journal of Medicine & Science in Sports, 32*(2), 359-371. https://doi.org/10.1111/sms.14079.

Keefe, P. R. (2021). *Empire of pain: The secret history of the Sackler dynasty*. Doubleday.

Keshishian, A., Greenberg, S. A., Agashivala, N., Baser, O., & Johnson, K. (2018). Health care costs and comorbidities for patients with inclusion body myositis. *Current Medical Research and Opinion, 204*(2-3), 1-16. https://doi.org/10.1080/03007995.2018.1486294

Lanz, T. V., Brewer, R. C., Ho, P. P., Moon, J.-S., Jude, K. M., Fernandez, D., Fernandes, R. A., Gomez, A. M., Nadj, G.-S., Bartley, C. M., Schubert, R. D., Hawes, I. A., Vazquez, S. E., Iyer, M., Zuchero, J. B., Teegen, B., Dunn, J. E., Lock, C. B., Kipp, L. B., … Robinson, W. H. (2022). Clonally expanded B cells in multiple sclerosis bind EBV EBNA1 and GlialCAM. *Nature, 603*(7900), 321-327. https://doi.org/10.1038/s41586-022-04432-7

Lotz, B. P., Engel, A. G., Nishino, H., Stevens, J. C., & Litchy, W. J.

(1989). Inclusion body myositis: Observations in 40 patients. *Brain, 112*(3), 727-747. https://doi.org/10.1093/brain/112.3.727

Lundberg, I. E., Fujimoto, M., Vencovsky, J., Aggarwal, R., Holmqvist, M., Christopher-Stine, L., Mammen, A. L., & Miller, F. W. (2021). Idiopathic inflammatory myopathies. *Nature Reviews Disease Primers, 7*(1), 86. https://doi.org/10.1038/s41572-021-00321-x

Mohannak, N., Pattison, G., Hird, K., & Needham, M. (2019). Dysphagia in patients with sporadic inclusion body myositis: Management challenges. *International Journal of General Medicine, 12,* 465-474. https://doi.org/10.2147/IJGM.S198031

Naddaf, E. (2022). Inclusion body myositis: Update on the diagnostic and therapeutic landscape. Frontiers in Neurology, 13, 1020113. https://doi.org/10.3389/fneur.2022.1020113

Naddaf, E., Shelly, S., Mandrekar, J., Chamberlain, A. M., Hoffman, E. M., Ernste, F. C., & Liewluck, T. (2021). Survival and associated comorbidities in inclusion body myositis. *Rheumatology*, keab716. https://doi.org/10.1093/rheumatology/keab716

Nelson, D. (2013). *The mystery of pain.* Singing Dragon.

Pongratz, D. E., Vorgerd, M., & Schoser, B. G. H. (2004). Scientific aspects and clinical signs of muscle pain. *Journal of Musculoskeletal Pain, 12*(3-4), 121-128. https://doi.org/10.1300/J094v12n03_17

Ramdharry, G., Morrow, J., Hudgens, S., Skorupinska, I., Gwathmey, K., Currence, M., … Machado, P. M. (2019). Investigation of the psychometric properties of the inclusion body myositis functional rating scale with Rasch analysis. *Muscle & Nerve, 60*(2), mus.26521. https://doi.org/10.1002/mus.26521

Rosenblum, A., Marsch, L. A., Joseph, H., & Portenoy, R. K. (2008).

Opioids and the treatment of chronic pain: Controversies, current status, and future directions. *Experimental and Clinical Psychopharmacology, 16*(5), 405-416. https://doi.org/10.1037/a0013628

Sadjadi, R., Rose, M. R., & Muscle Study Group. (2010). What determines quality of life in inclusion body myositis? *Journal of Neurology, Neurosurgery & Psychiatry, 81*(10), 1164-1166. https://doi.org/10.1136/jnnp.2009.183863

Schilling, J. M., Hughes, C. G., Wallace, M. S., Sexton, M., Backonja, M., & Moeller-Bertram, T. (2021). Cannabidiol as a treatment for chronic pain: a survey of patients' perspectives and attitudes. *Journal of Pain Research, 14*, 1241-1250. https://doi.org/10.2147/JPR.S278718

Schmidt, J. (2019). Endpoint choice for inclusion body myositis: A step too far? *The Lancet Neurology, 18*(9), 807-808. https://doi.org/10.1016/S1474-4422(19)30279-0

Shelly, S., Mielke, M. M., Mandrekar, J., Milone, M., Ernste, F. C., Naddaf, E., & Liewluck, T. (2021). Epidemiology and Natural History of Inclusion Body Myositis: A 40-Year Population-Based Study. *Neurology*, https://doi.org/10.1212/WNL.0000000000012004

Urits, I., Gress, K., Charipova, K., Habib, K., Lee, D., Lee, C., Jung, J. W., Kassem, H., Cornett, E., Paladini, A., Varrassi, G., Kaye, A. D., & Viswanath, O. (2020). Use of cannabidiol (CBD) for the treatment of chronic pain. *Best Practice & Research Clinical Anaesthesiology, 34*(3), 463-477. https://doi.org/10.1016/j.bpa.2020.06.004

White, C. M. (2019). A review of human studies assessing cannabidiol's (CBD) therapeutic actions and potential. *The Journal of Clinical Pharmacology, 59*(7), 923-934. https://doi.org/10.1002/jcph.1387

Živković, S. A., Gruener, G., Narayanaswami, P., & the AANEM Quality and Patient Safety Committee. (2021). Doctor–Should I get the

COVID -19 vaccine? Infection and immunization in individuals with neuromuscular disorders. *Muscle & Nerve, 63*(3), 294-303. https://doi.org/10.1002/mus.27179

APPENDIX: REPRESENTATIVE SIGNS AND SYMPTOMS OF IBM

Symptoms are what the patient feels and experiences; signs are what the doctor can see.

General issues

1) General fatigue—constantly feel very tired
2) Declining ability limits ability to work
3) Declining ability causes financial stress
4) Declining ability causes relationship stress
5) Declining ability causes intimacy issues

Muscles

6) Muscle wasting is obvious
7) Muscle soreness or pain present

Lower body

8) Swelling in the feet or ankles
9) Cramping/stiffness in the legs or feet
10) The toe doesn't lift high enough when walking, causing tripping
11) Problems stepping up onto a curb
12) Knees buckle or collapse, causing falls
13) Lose balance, causing falls
14) Problems getting up after falling
15) Problems getting up from a chair
16) Problems with stairs; climbing a ladder
17) Problems walking
18) Used, or now use: knee or ankle braces
19) Used, or now use: a cane
20) Used, or now use: a walker/rollator
21) Used, or now use: power wheelchair/scooter

Upper body

22) Drooping eyes
23) Drooping of the face
24) Slurred speech
25) Excess saliva/mucus
26) Neck weakness (hard lifting, turning head)
27) Problems raising arms over shoulders
28) Weakness in the wrists
29) Cramping/stiffness in

hands/arms

30) Problems with hand grip (holding a ball)
31) Problems using phones/computer
32) Problems closing fingers/making a fist
33) Problems writing/signing name
34) Problems with fine motor tasks (doorknobs, using keys, using scissors, picking up a needle)

Self-care/hygiene

35) Dependent on others to give pills/ medications
36) Problems washing/bathing
37) Problems independently dressing
38) Problems independently toileting
39) Dependent on others to wash and bath
40) Dependent on others to dress
41) Dependent on others for toileting

Travel

42) Problems traveling; flying, public transport
43) Problems using hotel rooms
44) Problems using public bathrooms
45) Problems eating in restaurants

Mobility/transportation

46) Need to use portable or ceiling lifts
47) Problems opening a car door
48) Problems getting in or out of a vehicle
49) Problems driving (regular vehicle)
50) Must be driven (modified vehicle/ handibus)

Problems sleeping / in bed

51) Physical problems getting out of bed
52) Problems turning over in bed
53) Problems sleeping
54) Need to use a specialized mattress/bed

Psychological

55) Declining ability causes psychological issues
56) Problems with anxiety
57) Problems with depression/suicide

Skin issues

58) Skin discoloration
59) Skin breakdown, pressure sores

Caregivers

60) Need daily help from partner/family
61) Partner/family caregiver has, or had, burnout
62) Need regular visits from a paid caregiver
63) Need a live-in, paid caregiver

Household

64) Need help cleaning, buying groceries, etc.
65) Need help doing banking

Eating

66) Problems opening food bags or jars
67) Problems using utensils, cutting food
68) Problems feeding self
69) Need someone to give food
70) Problems swallowing or choking
71) Needed a feeding tube inserted

Breathing

72) Have breathing issues
73) Need a BiPAP (or CPAP) machine
74) Need a daytime (noninvasive) ventilator

ACKNOWLEDGMENTS

I deeply appreciate Dr. Steven Greenberg for his insight and comments, which significantly improved this work.

I would like to acknowledge the Myositis Support & Understanding organization for their support and encouragement in writing this work.

I would like to acknowledge Lynn Wilson, Emma Nicholson and Joe Sanchez for their valuable suggestions.

I would like to thank Chris Nelson for his diligent editing.

The cover photo depicts Rene Castaños standing over Lake Louise, Alberta.

ABOUT THE AUTHOR

Bill Tillier received a Bachelor of Science Degree from the University of Calgary and completed a Master of Science Degree at the University of Alberta. Upon graduation, he worked as a forensic psychologist for over 20 years before developing inclusion body myositis. Over the years, Bill maintained his interest in psychology and a theory of personality development called positive disintegration. He maintains websites on this theory and as well on inclusion body myositis. Bill is now retired, spending most of his time volunteering. In 2018, Bill published a book on positive disintegration, *Personality Development through Positive Disintegration*. Bill serves as Science Advisor on the Myositis Support & Understanding Research Team. Bill and Angela live in Calgary, Alberta.

Printed in Dunstable, United Kingdom

66279721R00087